Eating Awareness Training

Molly Groger

With a Preface by
THOMAS LEBHERZ, M.D.

SUMMIT BOOKS

NEW YORK

Eating Awareness Training is under no circumstances meant to supersede the instructions of your physician regarding specific food restrictions.

Copyright © 1983 by Molly Groger
All rights reserved
including the right of reproduction
in whole or in part in any form
Published by SUMMIT BOOKS
A Division of Simon & Schuster, Inc.
Simon & Schuster Building
Rockefeller Center
1230 Avenue of the Americas
New York, New York 10020
SUMMIT BOOKS and colophon are trademarks of Simon & Schuster, Inc.
Designed by Eve Kirch
Manufactured in the United States of America

1   3   5   7   9   10   8   6   4   2

First Edition
Library of Congress Cataloging in Publication Data
Groger, Molly.
Eating awareness training.
1. Reducing—Psychological aspects.   2. Ingestion—
Psychological aspects.   3. Awareness.   I. Title.
RM222.2.G73 1983   613.2′4′019   83-4801
ISBN 0–671–46887–1

To My Father

I wish to express my sincere appreciation to Marilyn Bowden, Lois Gibson, and Linda Gross for their contributions to this book.

And my very special thanks to Sheri Groger for all her time, effort, knowledge and support.

CONTENTS

PREFACE

Over the years, literally hundreds of diet books and plans have been published. But the very fact that new ones continue to be published on a monthly basis demonstrates their failure to assist in weight control. Indeed, it has been impossible to find a text that goes to the heart of the matter, dissects the problem intelligently, and offers a safe, effective solution. Nevertheless, I'm pleased to announce that Molly Groger has accomplished all these things in *Eating Awareness Training*.

Eating Awareness Training is a delight to read; more importantly, it offers a workable method that one can easily follow to accomplish and maintain that all-too-elusive objective—*ideal weight*.

Through EAT, Molly Groger shows her readers how to reclaim what she calls their "birthright," the right to eat without compulsion, obsession or suffering. She provides a breakthrough program of eating what the body wants, as much as it wants, whenever it wants. The six-week plan is logical, clear and effective, and the personal feedback sections should prove very helpful to anyone following this program.

Nowhere in this book will you be burdened with

special diets, calorie counting or pill taking. Rather, you will be given an insightful discussion of the problem of abnormal eating, and through body awareness and a stimulating, practical plan, a *permanent* solution to your weight problem.

THOMAS B. LEBHERZ, M.D.

INTRODUCTION

A Little About Me

Five years ago I lost sixty-five pounds that I have been able to keep off, effortlessly—without diet or exercise—because I NO LONGER HAVE A WEIGHT PROBLEM.

When I was a little girl my mother was always extremely proud of what "a good eater" I was. That meant I ate anything and everything that was put in front of me (and whatever I could get on the side). A mother's dream . . .

But by the time I was fourteen, the dream had become a nightmare. I was taking reducing shots and pills, trying somehow to shrink the bulk that my adorable baby fat had become. And that was only the beginning of a long and frustrating battle against my body. I tried every new diet, theory and plan that promised to get me down to a normal size. And almost all of them worked.

But you know the rest of the story. . . . Each time I lost enough weight to get into my "thin clothes" and to bask in the compliments and envy of my friends, I would have my first "treat" and start the climb right back to the top. Every time! And every time I saw the pounds falling off, I swore I would not let it happen again; not *this* time, not after so much hard work and deprivation. *This* time, I would stay thin. Wrong!

In the best of circumstances, I don't like being a statistic. But there I was, according to national statistics, one of the typical 98 percent of the people who diet, lose weight, and gain it all back again and maybe even then some! After thirty-five years of dieting under what seemed like every regimen imaginable, I was still weighing in, with my five-foot two-inch frame, at a hefty one hundred eighty-five pounds—and still performing like the good little girl at my mother's table by eating everything in sight. If a friend called for dinner after I'd already eaten at home, I would never think of turning down the invitation. I'd just go out and eat a second dinner. Once, when I was trying to be efficient, I cooked enough food for three days so I wouldn't have to cook when I got home from work. That plan looked good on paper, but I ate all three dinners the same night I cooked them.

A New Look at the "Weight Problem"

I finally reached the point where I felt confronted with a life choice: diet forever or be fat. I vowed I would never diet again. I resented playing the yo-yo game, arduously working off pounds only to fly back to blimp proportions again. I resented such dismal edicts as "Change your eating habits" or "For the rest of your life you're going to have to watch yourself." I was fed up. So I decided to be fat and happy!

But have you ever tried to live *that* contradiction?

Even if I could delude my mind into accepting my appearance, I could not fool my body. My health was surely being affected by the extra sixty-five pounds I carried around. All the predictable signs were there: higher triglycerides, elevated cholesterol, high blood pressure, low energy, not to mention the constant backaches.

Of course I knew I could shed the extra pounds if I

really wanted to. I certainly had proven that to myself more times than I cared to remember. But for how long? Eliminating weight didn't seem to be the real problem. What I really wanted was to get rid of the weight problem. I wanted to be one of those blessed people who could eat whatever they wanted, whenever they wanted, and still keep their natural shape. I wanted to live my life with the freedom and enjoyment of a person without a weight problem.

I had a friend who used to call me at odd hours to see if I would join him for a hamburger, claiming that he was starved. We'd meet at a restaurant and both order hamburgers and french fries. Sometimes he would finish it all, sometimes only half, and sometimes he would eat only three or four bites and then push his plate aside. This kind of behavior was not within my realm of comprehension—or activity.

"You're really crazy," I'd tell him. "You acted as though you were starving and then you didn't even finish all your food."

He would shrug and say, "I've had enough. I'm comfortable."

I chalked him up as a nut and proceeded to clean my plate—and his. Within a year I gained forty pounds. He remained trim as ever.

Although his behavior seemed bizarre to me at the time, I later began to see the logic of it. If I could re-educate myself to eat like my friend, to respond to my *body's* hunger and comfort rather than to a variety of obsessions and ingrained patterns—if I could eliminate the *weight problem*—I could eliminate the weight. I could eat what I wanted, when I wanted, and would never have to worry about the weight gain/weight loss syndrome again.

And, in fact, that's what Eating Awareness Training has accomplished for me. I no longer have to choose between dieting forever or staying fat. I no longer have to give up the pleasures of eating. I have discovered a miraculous third alternative that is as available to you as it is to me.

What Is Eating Awareness Training?

You can completely eliminate cigarettes from your life; you can completely eliminate alcohol from your life; you can completely eliminate drugs from your life; but you cannot completely eliminate food from your life.

Nevertheless, many overweight people who have struggled for years with diets have come to the conclusion that eating is "bad" and not eating is "good." But eating is neither bad nor good. Eating has a rightful place in our lives—it is a natural function through which we nourish the body, and I can think of no reason why it should not be a pleasurable experience. What we want is the freedom to eat when it is natural to eat, to enjoy what we choose to eat, not what we think we "should" be eating; to know when the body needs food and when it is satisfied.

A Zen Master says: "Wise man eats when hungry—sleeps when tired."

And it really *is* that simple.

Eating Awareness Training or EAT is fundamentally a *learning* process. It teaches us to listen to the inherent wisdom of the body. In the context of EAT, learning is not the ability to memorize new theories; it is experience. It is the process of giving your body the chance to express its potential. It is a chance to get out of your own way and let the *real* you come out. You will learn to close the gap between the natural potential of your body and the way it has performed up to now.

And it really *is* that simple.

"Yes, but not for me. I'll always have a weight problem."

14

"Yes, but you don't understand, I eat from frustration" (or boredom, or loneliness, or anger).

"Yes, but everything I eat turns to fat. I hardly eat a thing and look at me. I just can't eat like other people."

"Yes, but I've tried everything and I'm just too undisciplined. I can't stick to anything."

"Yes, but I've been fat my whole life!"

"Yes, but I love to eat—food is too important to me. I don't want to give that up."

"Yes, but I'll never be thin enough to look good anyway. I'm just not built that way."

"Yes, but I already know why I am overeating—you can't help me."

"Yes, but most of my social life revolves around eating."

"Yes, but I don't need this. All I have to do is get back to: (a) exercising three times a week; (b) my good eating habits; (c) my low-carbo diet; (d) cutting out sugar; (e) all of the above. I know how to do it, I just have to get my head together. I'll get back to it next week."

"Yes, but . . ."

Sound familiar?

These are just some of the typical reactions of those who hear about Eating Awareness Training for the first time. Some go on to do the program and eliminate their weight problem. Others go on inventing excuses.

We all like to believe that we have a unique problem. It is sometimes easier to believe that the problem cannot be solved. That way we don't ever have to do anything about it.

But chances are your problem is not unique. The fact is:

ANYONE WHO IS NOT IN HIS OR HER NATURAL
SHAPE IS EATING FOR SOME REASON OTHER
THAN HUNGER

Eating Awareness Training teaches you to eat only when you are hungry and to stop when you are comfortable. As a result, you will melt, permanently, into your natural shape.

I recently heard a statistic on the news that revealed that the American public spends more money each year on new ways to lose weight than the whole of the medical establishment spends on research. And yet for all the money spent on weight control, it has been an exercise in futility for most. There is still a dismal 98 percent failure rate. But I never have to look for new ways to lose weight again, and if you follow the program outlined in this book, you won't either.

This is not a diet book. It contains no menu plans; no calorie/carbohydrate counter; no magic chemical combinations of food; no theories about fat cells or other excuses for why you can't lose weight; no methods to create aversions to foods you like; no affirmations to recite; no modification of behavior by practicing "good" eating habits, rewarding yourself for losing weight or learning to "think thin." Unlike other diet *and* no-diet books, in this one you will not find a word about "fattening" foods or sample meals, or foods you "should" or "shouldn't" eat. That's between you and your body. I will simply offer techniques that will enable you to perform as you were meant to—as an individual without a weight problem.

Why Diets Fail

A doctor was recently quoted in a national magazine as saying, "If diet books really worked, we'd be a nation of thin people." That is a conclusion I have come to myself, and I see it constantly reinforced by the steady stream of obese clients who say things like, "Weight Watchers really worked for me" or "I've been on a dozen different diets—all of them worked." Does that make any sense? It does if all you're concerned about is the temporary elimination of pounds. But, obviously, it doesn't do much to eliminate your weight problem.

Diets work only temporarily because they interfere with the natural instinct and potential of the body. Diets involve *control*.

"Control" is one of my least favorite words. It means I am doing something I don't want to do or not doing something I really want to do. Control produces tightness, which is a tremendous interference with natural potential. Every time we tell the body when, how much, what and why it should eat, we interfere with its natural processes. EAT shifts the responsibility for eating from the *mind* to the *body*—where it belongs. The body does not need to be controlled. It needs to be *trusted*. The body is entirely capable, by itself, of knowing how to eat.

I can hear some of you saying at this point, "My body's instincts are to eat everything I shouldn't and I would end up weighing three hundred pounds if I followed them." But that feeling comes from having listened to messages of the mind—*not* the body. (When I refer to the mind, I do not mean the brain, but rather the "crazymaker" that never stops telling us what we should or shouldn't do, what is right and what is wrong, and that keeps nagging us with "ideas" that sabotage our learning and performance.) Most of us have very little experience with how the body can perform. We keep stumbling over our minds. This is one area where it pays, as Fritz Perls says, to "lose your mind and come to your senses." This book is about learning to trust the body and giving it the chance to perform its miraculous functions.

The diet syndrome is a negative setup that preconditions us to failure. Each new diet plan we attempt, that "works for a while," reinforces our past experiences of failure to keep the weight off. And *this* is the process that is accepted as natural—a sad fact of life.

People constantly ask me, "Are you still on the program?" People are too used to thinking in terms of "on" and "off." "On" means we are on one diet program or another, being "good," suffering some form of deprivation. "Off" means we are not dieting, we are being "bad," feeling guilty, eating again and, as a result, failing to keep the weight off. Obviously we are setting ourselves up for failure. It is no wonder we have a hopeless feeling and develop a "what's the use" attitude that dooms us to being heavier than we have to be. I no longer have anything to be "on" or "off." *I do not have a weight problem!* I eat when I am hungry and stop when I am comfortable. I pay attention to what my body wants to eat and as a result, stay in my natural shape. I feel complete freedom with regard to eating.

Unlike *diets* where you lose twenty pounds in twenty days and gain them back in what seems like the next twenty minutes, EAT is not a crash program. Instead, it is an opportunity for you to melt into your natural shape at a pace which is natural for *your* body—and it keeps you there.

Looking for "Miracles"

It seems that every year there is a new "miracle" on the market that is touted as the answer to losing weight. These miracles have included such things as: pills to suppress the appetite; liquid-protein fasts; pills that block starches and fats. Some of these miracles have to be taken off the market almost as soon as they appear. Others take a little longer to be proven either harmful, ineffective or, at best, temporary. It is always interesting to me to learn what investigators will say next year about this year's current miracle.

We keep looking for miracles when there is nothing

more miraculous than the human body, and I can't imagine deliberately ingesting anything that interferes with its natural processes. The body is too precious to experiment with and that is why Eating Awareness Training makes so much sense. Can you imagine the Surgeon General issuing the following warning:

> "After extensive tests, nine out of ten doctors say, 'Stop paying attention to your body immediately. Listening to its messages may be harmful to your health.'"

Where Did We Go Wrong?

How has it happened that so many Americans have become bulimic; anorectic; willing to undergo such mutilating operations as stomach bypasses or stomach staplings; ready to have their jaws wired shut or to fast for months on end on an instant liquid or powder; or to become compulsive dieters, or at the very least, constantly confused and distracted by not knowing what, when or how much to eat?

Having been born with the potential to know when to eat, how much to eat, what to eat, and why to eat, where did we go wrong? How did we lose touch?

As human beings, we all have a unique tendency to interfere with our own potential. Where eating is concerned, that potential is interfered with from the moment we are born.

When I was born, it was a status symbol to have a plump baby. Success as a mother was measured, in large part, by the number of fat creases on the baby's body. Anything less than roly-poly was considered a sign of maternal failure.

As newborns we are put on eating schedules that regulate the times we are fed and what and how much we "should" eat. If a baby spits something out of its mouth the mother shoves it right back in.

Besides nourishment, food begins to serve a secondary

function in the baby's life. It becomes a placater. It's a rare mother who doesn't carry around a sack of food to quiet the child when it screams for attention or love. At the first sign of discomfort, a cookie is quickly stuffed into its mouth. The modern mother who has learned much about nutrition often does the same thing—only with rice cakes instead of Oreos. By the time a little person is old enough to feed itself, it has learned that stuffing something into the mouth is the way to handle many of its needs.

As we grow up, the mass media help to create even more misconceptions about the natural place of food in our lives, perpetuating and elaborating upon what we have learned as children. Take a look at excerpts from a few television commercials.

"Nothin' says lovin' like somethin' from the oven. . . ."

What a depressing thought! And how well it reflects the attitude a lot of us have: hand on the refrigerator door to cure our hurts and fulfill our longings for love.

"Bake someone happy. . . ."

I sure hope that's not my only resource.

"If you want to say you're sorry and don't know how—say it with a bundt cake."

In this scenario a little girl, holding a broken and dismembered doll, comes into the house sobbing bitterly. All she wants is a little compassion. What does she get? A bundt cake shoved in her face.

Small wonder we're a nation of overweight people. "Betcha can't eat just one!" "Aren'tcha hungry?" Stuff something into your mouth, the TV tells us constantly, and all will be well. Treacherously, it also teaches us that the svelte shall inherit the earth. A commercial urging you to eat mounds of food is quickly followed by one showing a tall, beautiful girl, weighing about forty-two pounds, wearing jeans that look like they have been painted on her.

EAT Is for Eaters

Eating Awareness Training is for anyone who eats—not only the overweight. It is for those who have more or less maintained their shapes but are tired of "watching" what they eat; it is for those who are in a perpetual knot over nutritional contradictions such as last year's good health tips having become this year's taboos; it is for anyone who wants to enjoy eating with freedom.

Eating Awareness Training is designed to eliminate interference to our natural potential.

The first reaction of many people is that this is too good to be true. "How can *I* ever eat what I want, when I want, and stay in my natural shape?" We are so conditioned to suffer over this problem that the simplicity of the answer seems unbelievable. I don't ask that you believe. I ask that you entertain the thought that this *is* possible. When you learn what your body really wants, you will be able to do it. You can be a person without a weight problem. You can be a freedom-eater. Make the commitment to follow this program for the next six weeks. Your own experience will be your teacher and your proof.

EAT—How to Do It

The subject of EAT is eating—eating as is your birthright: without suffering, without obsession, without compulsion, without anxiety about food or weight. EAT is about eating with freedom and a great deal of enjoyment; and it is by letting the body, rather than the mind (which is cluttered with theories and concepts), take responsibility for eating, that this is accomplished.

There are four ways to approach eating: in terms of *when, how much, what* and *why*. If you do this program one week at a time, by the sixth week you will have experienced *when* it is natural to eat, *how much* your body wants to eat, *what* it wants to eat, and *why* it wants to eat. That's what being without a weight problem is all about. And it comes with paying attention to the body instead of the mind.

Basic Ingredients of Eating Awareness Training

The basic ingredients of EAT—Trust, Staying in the Present, Attention Without Interference, and Amnesia—will teach you to become a freedom-eater. You will notice that they appear throughout the book.

Trust

Trust in itself is not a virtue. We need to trust what is trustworthy. When it comes to eating, the only thing that is completely trustworthy is one's own body.

The human body is a miraculously precise and complex creation. It is capable of carrying out, simultaneously, thousands of sophisticated functions, most of which you are probably not even aware of (i.e., your body can breathe, pump blood, kill germs, all at the same time)! And yet we treat the body as though it knows nothing about eating.

Just think of how much the body attends to without external instruction. No one runs out to buy the newest books with titles like "50 New Methods of Red Cell Production"; "Waste Elimination: A Modern Approach"; or "How To Construct a Baby Without Really Trying." So rather than waste time with theories, why not trust in and listen to the source itself—the body.

Numerous studies have been conducted in which very small children have been allowed to pick whatever foods they wanted to eat from conveyor belts. The results of the studies show that although it seemed the children were eating erratically (which means their diets didn't fit someone else's concept of what they should eat and would probably drive the average mother to distraction), after a month of total food freedom, they had selected a diet that was well balanced and healthy for them.

If you want to become a person without a weight problem, learning to trust the body is essential. It is also essential to learn to ignore the mind.

There are places that charge vast sums of money to help you "overcome" your cravings. Several of my clients had already tried some of their methods. They were made to bring in their favorite food, chew it up, spit it out and then eat it again, in order to create an aversion to the foods they craved. Yuchhh! And how about the programs that teach you to visualize cockroaches in your popcorn or ice cream so you won't want to eat them again? Double Yuchhh!

What we actually need to learn is, first, how to identify our cravings, and then, how to satisfy them—cravings of the body, not the mind. EAT will help you recognize the difference between the two. As we learn to trust the body, we will also learn to trust its cravings. It really does know what it wants to eat.

The Catch-22 of the overweight person is, "I eat when I'm depressed and I get most depressed when I diet."

Conversely, on this program, as you begin to trust your body you will begin to recognize its messages. Your trust will increase and you will recognize more messages. Your trust will increase even more and you will recognize even more messages.

Staying in the Present

Stay in the present. You will read that line over and over in this book. This is one of the most important techniques for learning and performance, and for enjoying what is happening to us now. (Have you ever looked at a plate that had been full of one of your favorite foods and not remembered tasting it as you gobbled it down?) Fixation on the past or future is one of the strongest interferences with learning, performance and enjoyment. Concepts of the past and speculations about the future keep us from really seeing what is happening to us now. We need to stay in the present as much as possible. Past and future are illusion. Now is reality.

When the water of a lake is very still, it is possible to see the bottom clearly. If we throw pebbles into the lake, it makes ripples that distort the clarity. The same is true of life situations. Concepts of the past and thoughts of the future are like ripples in the lake of clarity. To see clearly "what is" now, we need to eliminate those distractions and stay in the present.

As a dividend, learning to focus our attention on the present will enhance every aspect of our lives. It is truly amazing to discover, through the practice of keeping our attention on what is happening right now, how much habits and concepts (focusing on the past) and wishful or fearful thinking (focusing on the future) rob us of the experience we're having right now.

Attention Without the Interference of Judgment

Human beings have a highly developed learning skill at their disposal: the ability to focus attention. But attention is not constructive if it is distorted by judgment. It is attention *without* judgment that is valuable.

Notice the judgment words that so often infiltrate our thoughts and speech. Words like good, bad, should, shouldn't, right, wrong, ugly, pretty, fat, thin, alert us to the fact that we are creating ripples in the lake of clarity. How to eliminate that interference is dealt with in subsequent chapters.

The accurate feedback of "what is" without interference is essential to the body in order to make necessary changes quickly, effortlessly and naturally.

Amnesia

In future chapters I will ask you to practice amnesia—to disregard all your previous ideas about food and eating. I strongly urge you to forget what you know about calories, carbohydrates, fattening or unfattening, healthy or unhealthy. Forget about what you like, what you don't like, what you usually do, when you usually do it, how you usually do it, etc.

There is an old saying about learning: If you want to fill your cup with fresh clear water, you must first empty it of the old dirty water.

Perhaps the reason a child learns so easily in the first five years of its life is that a young child has had less time to clutter its mind with theories and concepts and therefore approaches new things like an empty vessel.

Erase the blackboard in your mind which is layered with all your theories, charts and opinions about diet and eating, at least for the next six weeks. On this clean slate the messages of the body can be inscribed clearly, and learning can happen quickly and effectively.

Amnesia will help you to learn about your body's messages as quickly and naturally as a child.

What Part Does Exercise Play in Eating Awareness Training?

Quite simply: none!

My feeling is that exercise should never be considered a means of weight control. Exercising to keep calories "burned off" creates the same illusion as does dieting. It will work only temporarily (if at all) and will more often than not lead to failure. Also, the practice of overeating and then relying on exercise to get rid of calories is abuse of the body. I know people who spend hours each day working out to lose weight. I often wonder what would happen to them if they broke a leg and couldn't follow their normal routine. They would still have to eat. Would they blow up like a poisoned dog?

It's obvious, however, that the body was created to move. That's why it has so many moving parts (although many of us seem to have forgotten that). You may find that your body, as it starts to melt, will begin giving you messages that it wants to move more. Pay attention to these messages. They are as trustworthy as the messages about hunger and comfort. Look for ways in your daily life to move the body more and more as it lets you know what it needs . . . *not* for weight control, but for your own good feeling. While working around the house and yard you might want to bend and stretch whenever possible. If your destination is within a few floors, you might want to take the stairs instead of the elevator. You can stop driving around for fifteen minutes looking for a place to park right in front of where you are going; walking a few blocks won't hurt your body. Walking is also a marvelous way to see a new city.

Although exercise is no substitute for this program, and should not be used as a crutch, it can certainly be advantageous to muscle tone, as a means of improving the cardiovascular system, and for relieving physical, mental and emotional stress. There is an enormous amount of material available on the relationship between exercise and health. You might want to consult your physician about the best plan for you.

Going Forward with Eating Awareness Training

The program outlined in this book is divided into six week-long sections. Read the book *one week at a time* and practice the lessons for a full week before going on to the feedback for that week and the next week's lesson. I cannot stress the importance of this enough. Give your body a chance to experience what your mind *thinks* it grasps immediately. Your experience is your teacher.

You might want to form a group with others doing EAT and meet after each week's lesson to discuss your experiences together. Or maybe not. It's up to you.

I advise you not to judge your progress either in relation to yourself or others. Be patient. The minute most people begin to diet they become obsessed with how much they have lost. You won't melt fifty pounds away in the first week of this program—it might not even be five pounds. But even if you were to melt as little as one pound a week until you reached your natural body weight and then stayed there forever without sacrificing the enjoyment of eating whenever and whatever you wanted— wouldn't you be satisfied? This is natural learning. It is not a temporary solution; it is a lasting one. Instead of being "relatively painless," it is fun.

Becoming a person without a weight problem is exciting. It is an adventure full of discovery. Relax, and let it happen to you.

WEEK 1

Awakening to the Body

In the past, I would often brag that I could eat anything, as much as I wanted, at any time, and never feel uncomfortable. What I have since discovered (to my initial chagrin) is that my body was not immune to discomfort. Its messages were merely drowned out by my mind.

But the body should not be ignored. In the course of a lifetime, friends, lovers, jobs, money, parents and even children can come and go. But when the body goes—what's left?

The first week of Eating Awareness Training is dedicated to the rediscovery of our bodies because the more attention we give the body, the better it will perform.

Relaxation Techniques

Learning to trust the body is the most essential part of becoming a person without a weight problem. Before we can learn to trust the body, however, we have to be able to *feel* it. Tension interferes with our ability to feel our bodies. Remember, this is not a crash course, and there are no tests or exams to cram for, so relax. The more we eliminate tightness and anxiety, the easier it is to open channels of communication with the body.

Before reading further, take a survey of your body. Are your shoulders hunched and tense? Is your stomach cramped? Are your fingers rigidly clenching this book? Are your teeth clamped tightly together? Is your breathing slow and relaxed or is it shallow? Unfortunately we have come to associate learning with tension, but tightening up does not enhance learning; it interferes with it. Relax and let learning happen.

Here are some very simple relaxation techniques:

Neck Rolls

First, close your eyes, and, sitting with your spine straight, but not rigid, drop your head forward onto your chest. Then rotate it very slowly in as wide an arc as comfort will permit. Do this four or five times in clockwise and counterclockwise directions.

Muscle Tensing

Now, starting with your feet and working up, tighten each area of your body, one part at a time, to its maximum degree of tension, and then quickly and completely let go, allowing a few moments to experience the increasing sense of relaxation. Then tense your entire body and let it go suddenly limp all at once. (It's advisable to do this sitting or lying down. Otherwise, going limp all at once can be hazardous to your limbs.)

Breathing

Finally, close your eyes and slowly take three deep breaths.

Try any or all of these simple techniques whenever you feel tension building up in your body.

Body Awareness

Standing up, with your eyes closed, focus your attention on the various parts of your body until you really *feel* them. Start with your feet. Then, one area at a time, move up to your calves, thighs, hips, stomach, chest, arms, shoulders, chin, neck and face. Take enough time to really feel that each of these parts of your body belongs to you.

Being conscious of the body in this way may be a new experience for you and may take a little practice. And for those who are used to ignoring their bodies it may result in anything from self-consciousness to revulsion. Or you may feel pleasantly surprised. But this technique is not for the purpose of judging yourself. Its only intention is to increase awareness of the body. Relax and keep practicing until you can really feel by focusing attention.

The next step is to feel your body with your hands. Feel your thighs, stomach, chest, arms, shoulders and face with your hands. How closely did feeling with your attention match what you felt with your hands? Are you surprised at what your stomach actually feels like? Does it feel larger, smaller, or in some other way different from the way it felt with your attention?

Notice what the mind is telling you about the body, "I hate my stomach . . ." "My thighs could be worse . . ." "I didn't know my chin was that fat . . ." "Ugghhh! . . ."

Now dismiss all judgments of the mind and feel again what is there. It's not bad or good; it's yours and it's there.

Where Am I?—Where Am I Going?

On this journey of becoming a person without a weight problem, you need to know where you are to begin with, and where you are headed.

Where Am I?—My "Now" Body

You have already begun your journey to becoming a person without a weight problem by feeling your body. Now take a look.

Stand naked in front of a full-length mirror and see your body as it actually is. For some, this may be difficult at first. Overweight people often have a tendency to hide things (like food—and feelings) and to shy away from really looking at themselves. Sometimes when they accidently catch a glimpse of themselves in a mirror or a store window, their eyes "run away" with panic and disgust. Mine certainly used to. So it may be hard in the beginning. But continue to make the effort to look at your body realistically, without judgments like: "It's ugly . . ." "It's hopeless . . ." or "It's really not that bad." Notice that these thoughts are entering your mind, and let them go. Turn your attention to the present. Judgments may enter your mind again. Notice them, let them go, focus your attention on the present. Keep doing this and soon the flow of judgments will clear and you will be seeing what really "is."

When a space shuttle malfunctions, veering off course, the control center doesn't scream, "You stupid space shuttle! Where the hell do you think you're going? You really blew it this time. I hate you!" The control center knows these judgments will not help matters. It simply gives the present coordinates and the desired coordinates, allowing the space shuttle to correct its course.

It's the same with judgments of the mind. The body needs accurate feedback in order to correct the situation —not condemnation or even praise.

Eating Awareness Training allows you to correct an error: the error of paying attention to the mind instead of the body where eating is concerned. Like the space shuttle, we need accurate information—relevant feedback. Words like "ugly," "beautiful," "fat," "lumpy" are irrelevant.

A lot has been written in recent years about accepting what you are, but there is a big difference between seeing yourself clearly and accepting yourself. I have run across too many large people who have learned what they call "acceptance" of their appearance. And that's their easy way out. They no longer have to do anything about a distorted body. They can accept it and stay the way they are.

There is no need to accept anything less (or should I say more?) than your natural shape. There is no reason to live with a problem that can be eradicated from your life. When I ask you to look at your body in the mirror, I am not asking you to accept what you look like. It is essential, however, that you know objectively what your body looks like.

Don't let the mind interfere with your learning. Don't let judgments—or acceptance—distort your perception of reality. It is beneficial to practice looking at "what is." Eliminate as much of the illusion as possible, and changes will occur quickly and naturally.

Look at the shape of your body as it is at least once a week for the next six weeks.

Where Am I Going?—My Natural Body

Everyone has a natural body, the one he or she was meant to have. I do not know what your natural body looks like, but something within you does. No matter how it has been distorted and abused, there is a natural shape in there, and you want to let it out.

The following technique will help familiarize you with your natural body.

Close your eyes and visualize what your natural body looks like without its superfluous weight. Remember, this is *your* natural body with *your* face on it. Don't imagine Raquel Welch's or Burt Reynolds's. Don't imagine yourself five feet eight inches tall if you are five feet two inches. Be realistic. Visualize the body you *can* have and were meant to have.

Picture what your natural body is wearing, what kind of setting it is in, what it is doing, how it is moving, how it is feeling. This is your real form, and it is attainable. Do not view it with anxiety, longing or tension. That would be as much a waste of time and energy as tearing up the map on your trip to Miami because you're angry that you're not already there. Become familiar and friendly with your natural shape. It's your birthright to have this body. It is rightfully yours. This is the one you will melt into, so learn to be comfortable with it.

Visualize your natural body several times a day.

Increasing Awareness of "What Is"

Many overeaters are compulsive; many are impulsive. We overeat for so many reasons that it would be an almost insurmountable task to deal with them one by one. By the time we got to the root of each and every problem, we'd be too exhausted to care. But we would have managed to divert our attention from doing something about our bodies.

We don't have to agonize over *why* we overeat in order to stop overeating. We just have to learn to trust in, and respond to, the remarkable organic computer that is programmed to know all about eating: the body. To help respond to that computer, we need to become conscious eaters. We need to focus our attention on the eating process.

Choices of Attention

The ability to focus attention is a valuable skill, and we have it at our disposal at all times. We always have the choice of where or on what to focus our attention. Focusing attention does not mean to strain, squint, try hard and tighten. That would be an interference. Focus attention in a relaxed manner—with necessary effort, but not the strain of *trying*.

Why Be a Conscious Eater?

When we become conscious eaters—when our attention to eating is increased without judgments and distractions

—the natural process of eating takes place. We eat when we are hungry, stop when we are comfortable, and begin to melt into our natural shapes.

Remember, we are not practicing behavior modification. Your body will modify your behavior, not vice versa. We do not want to have to "keep food out of sight," "avoid office snack machines," "arrive late to cocktail parties to avoid nibbles," etc. I once overheard a woman saying, "I know how to stay thin—eat only what you hate!" That, to me, sounds like a wretched way to live.

Eating Awareness Techniques

The following techniques are not meant to teach you how to avoid food or how to avoid the foods you enjoy. They are simply meant to increase your awareness of *what is happening in the present* so that your body can learn to make the choices necessary to attain its natural shape. These techniques need only be followed until the body takes responsibility for eating away from the mind. The stronger the commitment you make to these techniques, the faster the body can take over.

1. Whenever you want to eat, take the food to a table, sit down and close your eyes, take three or four deep breaths, relax the mind and body.

    This means *every* morsel of food, whether it is one peanut, one cracker, or scraps left on plates in the kitchen. I am not telling you not to eat— just to sit down and take the time to know that you are eating.

2. Eliminate all the obvious distractions.

    This means turn off the TV, the radio, the stereo. Put all your reading material away.

    Notice the subtle distractions of the mind (i.e., preoccupation with problems at work, ongoing projects, plans, etc.) They can take you just as far away from the present as the more obvious distractions (of TV, radio and conversation).

3. Devote *all* your attention to the food while you are eating.

If you are at work, be sure you stop all work activity, including the phone, when you eat. If you are dining with someone, when you want to talk, put the fork down and talk. When you want to eat, put all your attention on eating.

4. Notice the speed with which you eat.

Don't try to eat faster or slower, just notice the speed at which you eat. Trying to change creates tightness, which interferes with natural learning. But don't fall into the trap of *trying* not to try. Relax, let go and focus your attention where it needs to be. As you learn to trust your body, you will experience that it really does know what to do. Just give it a chance.

5. Notice the point at which you feel comfortable—not full.

I am not telling you to stop eating. Just pay attention to how the body is feeling at different times during your meal or snack.

6. If you are not hungry, you can choose not to eat.

What a unique idea! This might not happen in the first week, but I list it here because, believe it or not, in a short time it will be a distinct possibility.

In the beginning, use these techniques for *every* morsel of food that goes into your mouth. If you pass the refrigerator and open it to reach in and take something out, be sure you bring the food to the table, sit down, relax the mind and body, reduce distractions, focus all your attention on eating, and notice when you are comfortable. If you open the cupboard and reach for one potato chip, take it to the table, sit down, relax the mind and body, reduce distractions, focus all your attention on eating and notice when you are comfortable. Sitting down does not include the driver's seat of your moving car. Putting your full attention on eating while you are driving may help eliminate your weight problem, but it could also eliminate your car, and maybe you. So wait until you can sit somewhere without distractions, or, if you must eat immediately, pull off the road, stop, and pay full attention to your eating.

Don't panic. This monitoring process will not continue for the rest of your life. It is part of the learning process. Perhaps you can remember other things you have learned in the past, like learning to walk or drive a car. What required complete attention in the beginning is now almost instinctive. When your body has taken back the responsibility for eating, you can do whatever you want and you will still know when you are hungry or comfortable. Your attention will automatically be where it needs to be.

"I Hardly Ate a Thing All Day"

A friend who was constantly battling weight used to say to me, "I don't understand why I can't lose weight. I fasted all day." I was very sympathetic until I spent one of those "fast days" with him. He continuously, unconsciously, put food into his mouth: a potato chip, a piece of candy, a carrot, a cookie, popcorn, crackers, a peanut-butter sandwich, an apple, one at a time, without ever sitting down. Toward evening, I suggested we go to dinner. His response was "Oh, no! I can't go to dinner. I'm fasting."

How many times have you heard yourself say, "I hardly

ate a thing all day." Just as we have become insensitive to the body's feelings, we have become unconscious of the food going into our mouths. We need to become aware that we are eating. To help increase that awareness, get a notebook and for the next six weeks keep a record of your food intake, setting up charts as follows:

TIME	ITEM	QUANTITY
8:00 AM	toast	1 slice
	butter	1 pat
	jam	1 spoon
	eggs	2
	coffee	2 cups
	sugar	2 spoons
	cream	1 tbsp
10:00 AM	peanuts	2
10:15 AM	peanuts	4

This chart is not intended for the purpose of counting calories or carbohydrates or even to analyze how much you eat. Do not judge what you eat. Judgments interfere with the messages of the body. Don't compare one day to another. Don't try to keep as clean a page as possible for the sake of denoting small intake. Don't use your notebook as a whip, lamenting over large numbers in the quantity column. It is not meant to be a diary of self-abuse. Creating a clean page will not solve your weight problem. Just record "what is." No one is going to go over your notebook with you and tell you how bad or good you were. When I work personally with clients, I never look at their notebooks. My seeing what is in their notebooks would not increase their awareness. This technique would be just as effective if you were to record your intake and then immediately throw the paper away. It is simply another tool, an important one, to increase your awareness of the eating process.

People who have taken behavior modification courses have asked me if they should record what they eat beforehand. But that would *not* be staying in the present. You don't know how much you are going to eat before you eat. Anything you decide before it happens is in direct conflict with the purpose of staying in the present and being in touch with what is happening now. You Cannot Tell The Body What To Do And Listen To Its Messages At The Same Time. That is a contradiction. This technique is not a trick to get you to eat less. Its only purpose is to increase your awareness of the eating process.

Timing

It is important to practice the techniques of Week 1 for *one full week* before reading further. Because most people are so used to being told what to eat and being judged for eating too much or the wrong things, it is difficult to understand, at first, that this program is so different. This is a learning process. You are learning to *trust your body*. You and your body will solve your weight problem. Cramming the information into your *head* all at once will not help eliminate your weight problem. You will learn from your experience. That is how change takes place. And if the experience is one you enjoy, such as having the freedom to eat whenever and whatever you choose, the change will become permanent—successful. So have the patience to read this book *one week at a time* and practice the techniques for one full week before going on. This is really crucial to your success. Your patience will be well rewarded.

I want to reiterate that these techniques are not being used to change your behavior and will not need to be practiced once your body takes responsibility for eating. At that time, there's no reason why you can't watch TV and eat at the same time and still know when your are hungry and when you are comfortable.

Your body is a precious gift. What could be more important for the next six weeks than putting your attention into a process that will help keep that body in its natural shape forever?

Make a strong commitment to follow the techniques offered in this book *one week at a time*. The commitment you make to Eating Awareness Training will benefit you for the rest of your life. It can be one of the most rewarding decisions you've ever made. You *can* attain your natural shape forever—without suffering, and without deprivation. It can be an exciting and enjoyable adventure. The benefits will be immeasurable. Imagine being a freedom-eater, being able to eat whatever you want, whenever you want, and being a person without a weight problem.

So have fun with your discoveries and realizations. Relax and allow natural learning to happen.

Homework For Week 1

- Look at your body in the mirror at least once a week, without judgments. *Know where you are.*
- Visualize your natural body three or four times a day. *Know where you are going.*
- Follow the Eating Awareness Techniques. Focus full attention on the eating process.
- Record your food intake in your notebook, without judging yourself. Increase your awareness of "what is."
- Practice the techniques offered here for *one full week* before reading further. It is essential to learn from your own experience, and experience takes time.
- Have fun rediscovering your body.

Feedback from
WEEK 1

When I meet with clients after their first week of practicing the techniques of awakening to the body, attentive eating and focusing on "what is," they are usually brimming with questions to be answered and experiences to relate. Here are some of the questions that most frequently arise, followed by my answers to them. Perhaps they may be questions that are on your mind as well.

Q. A lot of things went wrong this week—I felt so much pressure at work. I just couldn't do the techniques very often. It was a bad week to start. It's okay to go on to the second week, isn't it?

A. Eating goes on no matter what happens in your life. The body needs nourishment and knows when, how much, what and why it wants to eat. If you wait until "things are good" to start paying attention to these techniques, what will happen when things go "bad" again? When you are about to put food into your mouth, no matter what is happening, take it to the table, sit down, relax your mind and body, eliminate distractions and put all of your attention on the food. If you can't do that at the moment you

41

decide to eat, wait until you can. I am talking about just a few minutes a day. Those few minutes will not eliminate the pressures in your life, but they will help to eliminate your weight problem. To continue to abuse your body doesn't solve problems; it creates new ones. Don't let your mind's continuous excuses for why you cannot do this program delay your progress. The mind will never run out of excuses. When a client explains all the reasons why he or she has not been able to do the techniques of Week 1, it comes as a shock when I will not go on to the second week's techniques. There would be no point.

It is important to experience every aspect of this process in the order presented. It is the *experience* you have with your body that will eliminate your weight problem. Do not put this program in the same category as the others you have collected throughout your lifetime. This is not merely more information to feed into the mind. It is a permanent, experiential solution.

Whatever the reason, do not let an initial procrastination spoil the whole thing for you. Go back and do the first week again. Allow it to happen for you. It will be well worth your time.

Q. Most of the time I can eliminate distractions and be attentive to eating, but I have a great deal of difficulty when I eat breakfast because I'm so used to reading the morning paper at that time. What can I do?

A. When I meet with clients for the first time, so many of them tell me, "Eating is one of the most important things in my life," or "I love food and love to eat." If that's true, if it really is such a great experience, why can't eating be an activity unto itself? Think about some of the other great and joyful experiences of your life. Do you read a magazine or watch TV while partaking in those activities? Isn't eating an experience that can stand alone? Maybe you are not really aware of the place eating has in your life. Putting your full attention on the food will help you know whether you really want to eat or read the paper, and will increase the enjoyment of whichever activity you choose. Dividing your attention between eating and reading detracts from both. For these six weeks, make your choice—either eat or read the paper.

Q. I left my notebook at home one day. Is it all right to fill it in at the end of the day when I get home?

A. The purpose of recording your intake is to focus your attention on the present, when eating is actually happening. If you leave your notebook at home, you can always write on a piece of scratch paper. If you have no paper, write in your notebook mentally. Be sure to record every item mentally just as if your notebook were there. You don't have to act like an eccentric and whip out your notebook in the middle of a business luncheon or a dinner date—but the sooner you can record your intake after eating, the more aware you will become of the eating process.

Q. What about the movies? I always eat popcorn at the movies. That doesn't count, does it?

A. That question has been asked several times, once even by an attorney who seriously attempted to defend the position that popcorn at the movies isn't an eating activity—that it is a *movie* activity. Try to explain that difference to your body! Eating is eating. Movies are movies. For this next six weeks, if you are at the movies and want to eat popcorn or candy, take it to the lobby, sit down, relax your mind and body, reduce the distractions and pay attention to the food only. When the body has taken over the responsibility for eating, you will be able to watch the movie and still be conscious of your body's hunger and comfort. The goal of being permanently without a weight problem is worth the commitment to follow these techniques for a few weeks.

Q. How do I know this isn't my natural body?

A. This question was asked by a woman who was at least one hundred pounds overweight. Oh, how we'd love to think that we were meant to be this way. That certainly would absolve us of having to take any responsibility for changing things. Don't let this kind of delusion prevent you from attaining what is really yours.

Q. I was at a cocktail party and everyone was standing up. I really wanted to eat the hors d'oeuvres. But how?

A. Again, you don't have to act weird and take an hors d'oeuvre, dash to a chair, pop it in your mouth, spring up again and run back to where you were. If the situation is such that you *must* have whatever they are serving where they are serving it, stop, relax the mind and body, focus your attention on the food alone . . . and eat. This is to avoid the danger of unconsciously popping one hors d'oeuvre after another into your mouth without knowing what you are doing. I am not telling you not to have any of the goodies. I'm simply pointing out that this kind of situation is often a trap for unconscious eating.

Q. I'm a traveling salesman who usually eats lunch while driving from one customer to the next. Otherwise I wouldn't be able to eat until very late. How do I solve that one?

A. I'm willing to bet you will not faint behind the wheel if you delay eating from noon to three o'clock, let's say. Take a risk and wait until you get to your destination to eat. Then you can relax, eliminate distractions and pay attention to the food. Most people who are trying to solve their weight problem usually have enough bulk to sustain them for more than a two- or three-hour wait without the danger of starving to death. But sometimes hunger and deprivation can be frightening. So, if you absolutely cannot wait, pull over, stop your car, relax your mind and body, and eat.

Q. I lost three pounds this week. I don't understand why. I didn't try to diet. What's happening?

A. What's happening is that the body is beginning to make choices because you are allowing it to. You are giving it attention. For some, the body responds very quickly to that attention and changes begin to happen in the first week. For others it will take a little longer. The more attention you give the body, the faster it will begin to make choices. You really don't even have to understand. To analyze your experience can be a complication that interferes with learning. Remember, the body will go on functioning whether you understand it or not. You don't need to put everything in a little box. Trust, stay in the present and enjoy it.

Q. How long do I have to write down everything I eat?

A. The length of time necessary for the body to start taking over responsibility for eating varies with the individual. You are the only one who can tell when it is time to stop recording your intake. You are the only one who knows when you no longer need a tool to be aware of the eating process. When you know that you are ready, it is time to stop.

This is also true of the Eating Awareness Techniques. Although most people find it takes longer to remain aware of eating amid distractions, only you will know when you can watch TV and still be in touch with the body's signals.

Q. I can't get a clear picture of my natural body yet. What can I do?

A. Keep practicing in a relaxed manner. Don't strain or *try*, because the anxiety might cause interference. If the picture still doesn't come, see if you have a picture of yourself at a time when you might still have been in your natural body, or close to it. If that has never been the case, draw a picture or sculpt away the distortions on a current picture. The natural body will begin to reveal itself.

Q. How can I be sure I will like my natural body?

A. This question was asked by a man who was at least eighty pounds overweight—sixty of those pounds in the form of an enormous stomach hanging over his pants. Before I could frame a delicate answer, I heard myself say, "You've got to like it better than the one you're in now!"

Fortunately he laughed. This is just an example of the kinds of defenses the mind will present to try to keep you from using these techniques.

Q. The hardest thing for me to do this week was to look at myself in the mirror. I've been avoiding it for years. My figure disgusts me. I even have the mirror in the bathroom at an angle so that I can see only my face. I don't even have a full-length mirror in the house. Can't I forget about this one?

A. For years you have avoided looking at your body in the mirror because you have had no viable way to change it. It's painful to look at yourself objectively under those circumstances. Now you have a permanent solution at your disposal. Look at your body, without judgment, without that hopeless sinking feeling, but rather as a point of interest, to show you where you are at the moment.

Q. It's hard to keep from judging myself. Will that ever stop?

A. Looking at ourselves judgmentally is an ingrained practice. Instead, start looking at yourself with *interest*. To have interest in what is happening to your body is productive, to judge is an interference. When judgments appear in your mind, simply focus your attention on "what is." This is a skill you are learning, and practice makes perfect.

Q. How often should I weigh myself?

A. Weighing yourself can interfere with the process of eliminating your weight problem. What have your past experiences of getting on the scale done for you? If you gained weight, or didn't lose any, what an excuse that was for feeling miserable, having a lousy day and compensating by eating even more than the day before. And if you lost weight, what a marvelous excuse for eating a little bit more. Weighing does not change the shape of the body. When we put so much of our attention into results, we miss the experience of the present and it is what is happening "now" that will influence results.

If you are a scaleaholic—stop before you get on the scale and feel your body. Then see if the scale matches your feeling.

Q. At night I lie in bed and watch TV and like to snack. How do I handle that?

A. Very simply. You have the choice of continuing to watch TV without eating, or getting up, taking your snack to the table, following the Eating Awareness Techniques, and then going back to bed and watching TV. The choice is yours. If you decide to snack, that's fine—but it will be a *conscious* choice.

Q. What about alcohol? Is it okay to drink?

A. This is a question that frequently arises because many people have had the distressing experience of being on diets that restrict drinking because of the high caloric count of the alcohol and mix. In fact, one diet became very popular because it was touted as the "Drinking Man's Diet."

On this program and forevermore, you will not be on a diet—you will not be concerned about calories. However, you are going to want to be as aware—as conscious—as possible so that you can listen to the messages from your body. If you can remain aware and still drink, it will not interfere with the process. The danger of drinking to the extent that you are, figuratively, unconscious, is that you will also be unconscious of your body. You might want to start noticing what amount of alcohol becomes an interference to your awareness.

Q. Should I eliminate sugar? Maybe I should diet for a few weeks to get a "good start."

A. This is a good time to practice amnesia. Forget all about calories and carbohydrates, healthy and unhealthy, fattening and nonfattening—and dieting. All of these notions interfere with your ability to learn to trust your body. Respond to your body, not your mind. Have your attention in the present. You can't tell your body what to do and learn to listen to it at the same time. Dieting, and why it fails, has already been discussed. Let go of your diet consciousness.

Q. Wouldn't it help not to have ice cream or other goodies in the house so I'm not tempted? I usually do that when I want to lose weight.

A. Avoiding temptation and achieving freedom are two different things. When you are a person without a weight problem, it doesn't matter what is in the house. You will want to eat only when you are hungry. That's what Eating Awareness Training accomplishes. You will no longer have to trick yourself into avoiding temptation. You will be free.

Q. Do you ever gain weight and then have to watch yourself for a few days?

A. No, I never gain weight except for a temporary pound or two of water retention now and then, and yes, I always watch myself in the sense that I am aware of my body and its hunger and comfort. As a result, I am completely free to eat whatever and whenever my body wants.

I have never heard a legitimate excuse for eating unconsciously. Problem situations which, on the surface, seem to preclude one from following the techniques are easily dealt with upon closer scrutiny. The mind will come up with a million reasons to sabotage the body.

The following are some of the learning experiences and realizations my clients have had after the first week of Eating Awareness Training. Maybe you have had similar experiences.

"I always thought eating was the most important thing in my life. I thought I'd rather eat than do anything else. I was amazed that this week, more than once, I got bored with eating and stopped before I had eaten everything because I really wanted to watch TV. It was a mind-blowing experience for me. I already feel a touch of freedom about food. I never thought I would choose TV over food. Never!"

"This is the first time I ever started any weight-loss program and felt that nobody was taking anything away from me. I kept looking around for someone to tell me to stop eating this and stop eating that and even went back and read my notes to see if they said anything about what not to eat. I couldn't find anything like that. It certainly is a new experience for me, and it took a little getting used to."

"I never realized how many times I went to the refrigerator and ate standing up in front of it without being conscious of or tasting what I was eating. I never realized how much I ate while preparing dinner. I was one of those people who said, 'I hardly ate a thing all day.' I guess I thought eating while standing up in the kitchen didn't count. But this week it seemed like more trouble than it was worth, sometimes, to take the food to the table, so I actually found myself putting it back into the referigerator and going about my business. I didn't feel deprived because I knew I could eat it if I wanted to—it was just too much trouble. That's really not like me!"

"I can't believe what happened when I began to feel my body. For the first few days I felt that my body was very fragile, but then I realized that it was just *feeling* that was so new to me. It had been so long since I'd felt I had a body. It takes some getting used to. Toward the end of the week, I began to like the feeling of awareness. It's incredible, being a nurse, that I was able to ignore my body for so long!"

"I enjoyed eating this week more than I ever have before. Everything tasted so good. I thought I was really into it before, but I had been missing out on taste. Attention really makes a difference!"

"I'm such a creature of habit. I always read when I ate. This morning I realized that I spent the whole time I was eating reading the salt shaker—and all it said was 'S.'"

"I was amazed to find that several times this week I stopped eating before the plate was empty. I felt I had had enough. I really don't understand what's happening, but I know that I am already beginning to feel better. Just this one week seems to have made a difference."

One of the great reliefs is that you don't have to understand how this works. You just have to experience it. The body is a miracle in the way it functions and, given a chance, will take responsibility for eating and put it into its proper perspective. Just enjoy what is happening and don't be concerned about understanding it intellectually.

Go on to Week 2

WEEK 2

Hunger

The Difference Between the Urge to Eat and Hunger

When does the mind give us the urge to eat?

When we are:
    lonely
    sad
    happy
    bored
    anxious
    frustrated
    angry
    fearful
    insecure
When we:
    pass the refrigerator
    need a reward
    feel sorry for ourselves
    have worked too hard
    haven't worked hard enough
    don't like what we are doing

Because:
> it's time
> it's there
> it looks good
> it smells good
> it sounds good

When does the body want to eat?

WHEN IT IS HUNGRY!

And it really *is* that simple.

Hunger is a physiological signal that tells us the body wants nourishment. We have become such creatures of habit and confused mental messages that we give ourselves very little chance to experience hunger. A fifty-year-old woman told me that until she did EAT she had never given herself the chance to experience hunger. What most of us *do* experience so often is the "urge to eat."

One of the most important things you can get from Eating Awareness Training is the ability to recognize the difference between hunger and the urge to eat.

Hunger is very fickle, erratic and independent. It does *not* depend on the time of day, the amount of food on the plate, the social situation or the wish to please others. Hunger differs from day to day, hour to hour. It has no pattern. It would take an incredibly sophisticated computer to process all the data necessary to come up with when you should be hungry and how much food you need to ingest. We all have that ultimate computer with us at all times. It's called the body and it has the potential to tell us when it is hungry, when it is comfortable and when we are putting more into it than it wants, thereby distorting its shape and its ability to function to maximum potential.

Where the subject of eating is concerned, it is crucial to trust your body—the supreme authority. Trusting the body and its signals is essential to eliminating your weight problem.

Every time you *tell* the body when to eat, how much to

eat, what to eat, and why you should eat, you are not trusting its ability to maintain its natural shape. We have been taught to listen to everything spoken and written about diet and "proper" eating, and we have also been taught to totally ignore the only real authority on these subjects—the body.

The fact that dieting theories change from year to year, invalidating one another, doesn't seem to faze us. We keep expecting each new theory that comes along to be a panacea. Don't eat cholesterol. Cholesterol-free diets may cause cancer. Eat as much grapefruit as you can. Stay away from grapefruit—it is harmful to the kidneys. Eat one meal a day. Eat several small meals a day. These theories may sound right, but how many really feel right?

I'm not saying that all the concepts you hear are false. All I am saying is that they may have nothing to do with what your body wants at the moment. If you will start trusting the body, you won't have to figure out which concept is correct. Our sandard equipment will tell us how to eat.

This week we want to begin to give the body choices about eating—to give it a chance to perform for us. Given that chance, the body will choose the way of eating that is conducive to maintaining its natural shape and even its natural health.

How to Get in Touch with Hunger

There is an area of the stomach, somewhere near the waist, that tells you when you are hungry, when you are stuffed, and when you are somewhere in between.

Close your eyes and put your attention on that spot until you feel something relating to hunger and fullness. Then use the following scale of 0–10 to describe that feeling.

> 0 = very empty, very hungry
> 5 = just comfortable—satisfied without feeling stuffed.
> 10 = very stuffed, very uncomfortable

Notice your mind "helping" you arrive at a number with thoughts like "I can't be hungry, I just ate." Or "I haven't eaten all day, I guess I must be pretty hungry."

Now, turn your attention back on that hunger-level spot and *feel*. What number would you put on it right now? A 3, for instance, would be at a level where you could eat, but it would be okay not to. It would mean that you were not quite hungry enough to need to eat. If you are at a 7, you are more uncomfortable than your body wants to be.

Any time you eat to a feeling above a 5, you are feeding the mind, not the body, and will therefore distort the body's shape and abuse its health.

The body would be very happy if you didn't eat until you were at least a 2 and never ate above a 5. It would then melt down to its natural shape and stay there forever.

One of the most important techniques for eliminating a weight problem is to stay in touch with that hunger level, especially before putting anything into your mouth. Learn to trust it. In the beginning, your numbers may not be accurate, but you will become more familiar with the feeling and learn from your experience. If you think you are stopping at a 5 and you then feel uncomfortable, what you felt was probably a 7. If you feel you are stopping at a 4 or 5 and are not melting into your natural shape, your feeling of 5 is really a 6 or a 7. (Remember this is not a crash program. Your body will lose at its own rate and it will be a different rate for everyone.)

In this second week of Eating Awareness Training, I ask you to add a fourth column to your intake record entitled "Hunger Level." Mark down your hunger-level number when you start to eat and your hunger-level number when you finish eating. This includes every morsel that enters your mouth—even if it is one peanut. The chart would look something like this:

TIME	ITEM	QUANTITY	HUNGER LEVEL
12:00	eggs	2	
	toast	1 slice	
	potatoes	6 bites	1–5
2:00	peanut	2	3–5
4:00	peanut	4	4–5

One of the reasons to practice Eating Awareness techniques is to be able to *know* when a 4 or a 5 has been reached. At that point, put down the fork and give yourself a chance to experience what "comfortableness" is like. This might very well be a new feeling. We have become so used to chronic overeating that we have no idea what it feels like to be comfortable when we are finished eating.

It can be fun to experiment with these hunger levels. For instance, when you wake up, wait until you reach at least a 2 before you eat. Remember, one day that could be at 7:00 A.M. and the next day not until 5:00 P.M., or maybe not at all. One woman called me after three days and said, "I haven't been hungry yet. What should I do?"

Or you might take a couple of days and not eat above a 4. Take a risk! Put the fork down and see how the body likes that feeling. Every adventure requires some risks.

If there are times when you are not sure whether you are experiencing hunger, wait twenty minutes and see how you feel then. We have numbed the body so that it has not experienced the feeling of hunger for so long— either by overeating, fasting, dieting, or eating on schedule—that we have to learn all over again what we knew at birth.

The feeling of being light, while at the same time eating what you want, when you want it, is exquisite—and one that you will want to keep experiencing. That is how successful change takes place. My experience was that instead of resenting hunger I began to welcome it, and also the feeling of satisfying it. Eating enjoyment increases rather than decreases with EAT. The miracle of eating with freedom and melting into your natural shape begins to manifest itself.

Abuse

We've all heard a great deal in recent years about drug abuse, child abuse, and wife abuse. But what about the abuse of one's own body? We don't hear too much about that, but we certainly see a lot of it.

Abuse is defined as injury or improper use. What do we do to our bodies every time we eat when we are not hungry? And if "batter" is defined as abuse with successive blows, what should we call the relentless consistency with which we eat more than the body wants? It would seem we constantly abuse and batter our own bodies and, in so doing, distort their shape and ruin their health.

So each time we eat for some reason other than hunger and eat more than is comfortable we are abusing our bodies. We are not solving problems, we are creating them.

The "Clean the Plate" Syndrome

And now we come to a real biggie: The "Clean the Plate" syndrome or: "Did you make all gone?"; "It's a shame to waste it"; "This may be my last chance to eat!"; or yet another excuse, "At these prices I'm going to finish every last morsel!" (Another swell reason to distort your body.)

I recently had dinner with friends who have a four-year-old. When he finished his hamburger, the entire family descended on him with praise: "What a good boy!" "Grandpa, did you see, he finished his whole hamburger!" "You are wonderful, you are going to be so big and strong." "You did so well, you can have a candy bar."

I asked quietly, "What is so wonderful about his eating a whole hamburger?"

I was told, "Well, he usually doesn't eat the whole thing."

Then I said, "Maybe all those other times he wasn't hungry. What's really wonderful is that he knew when to stop."

There was a stunned silence. I had introduced something so foreign to their way of thinking that no one even knew how to react. I sadly realized I had been an eyewitness to the creation of another little person with a weight problem!

The "clean the plate" panic originates from messages like these: If we clean the plate we are a very good girl (boy) and will probably even get a reward—most of the time in the form of a gooey goody. Or the most famous of them all: "Children are starving in Europe." A nurse taking a child-rearing course had to fill out a questionnaire for class discussion that included the question "When should you start making your child eat all the food on his plate?"

Even though the average person with a weight problem has probably never come close to starving to death (except from a self-imposed diet or regimen), he or she typically acts as though each meal is the last, in a kind of panic that occurs at *every meal!* Some of these feelings come from the endless diets and deprivation—the mocking looks if we eat when we are not "supposed to," all of which make us want to eat as much as possible at every opportunity.

This panic about cleaning the plate will come to an end if you learn to trust your body. You will then have complete freedom to eat whenever you are hungry and therefore will not need to clean the plate or stuff yourself. It's not your "last chance." Food is accessible. Nobody is taking it away from you. If you are really hungry twenty minutes after eating dinner, you can feel perfectly free to finish what is on your plate or to eat something else. Remember, you are learning to trust your body. It will not betray you. It becomes perfectly all right, even natural, to stop eating, when your hunger is satisfied, wrap the food and put it in the refrigerator, or, if dining out, ask for a doggie bag and take it home. That is because you have permission to eat whenever and whatever you want. I have taken food home from the fanciest restaurants. As a matter of fact, I have an international cuisine in my freezer. I will not abuse my body to please my dinner companion, the waiter in the restaurant, or anyone else.

Remember

This is not permission to eat what the mind wants.
We are learning to trust the body. The mind is
not trustworthy.

Attention Without Judgment

If you eat above a 5, remember to be attentive to the feeling of your body at that time without the judgments that you have been bad or a failure or have done something wrong. These thoughts will greatly interfere with your chance to learn from your experience and keep you from feeling things as they are. All that really happened is that you ate to a 7. Now, what does that feel like? Experiencing that feeling gives you the feedback which allows your body to make the choices and changes it needs to make.

Amnesia

Practice amnesia. You don't know when you will get hungry or how much food it takes to make you comfortable. That is part of the adventure. Instead of *telling* the body what you think you know about eating, *listen* to its signals about hunger and comfort. Learn as a child might.

We are shifting the responsibility for eating from the mind to the body where it belongs. Your body will not betray you. Give it a chance. Take the risk! If listening to all those external theories had worked for you, you probably wouldn't be reading this book now.

Don't panic if it takes a small amount of food to satisfy you in the beginning.

After the first few weeks of EAT, some of my clients tell me, with concern, that it is taking very little food to satisfy them—to reach a 5. My experience is that very often, while the body is overweight, it takes less food to satisfy it, and after the body starts to melt away the food intake increases. This could be because while the body is happily eliminating weight it does not want to ingest as much as when it is closer to its natural shape. Of course, this differs from body to body. You have your own personal authority with you all the time: your own body.

Stay in the Present

"Mealtime," "portions," "allowed" and "supposed to" all work to obscure what is happening right now. *Stay in the present*. The decisions to eat and stop eating have to be made in the present. That's when hunger and comfort happen. The important thing is "What is my hunger level *right now?*"

When you are feeling that hunger level, observe your mind trying to give you reasons why you should be hungry or comfortable. These reasons have nothing to do with hunger and will interfere with your body's messages. Hunger is an experience that has nothing to do with the logic of the mind.

> Remember
> Don't look for new eating patterns.
> Stay in the present.

Don't think you did something wrong if yesterday you didn't get hungry until 3:00 P.M. but today you got hungry at 7:00 A.M. Hunger is erratic. My experience is that it has no pattern. You don't have to understand why. You just have to trust your body. People ask me all the time what I "normally" eat, or how many times a day I "normally" eat. There is no norm. It changes all the time. Besides, what *I* eat has nothing to do with *your* body; *my* body will stay the same no matter what *you* eat. It is *your* body that will eliminate *your* weight problem.

Relax, let go and let it happen for you.

Homework for Week 2

- Continue to follow Eating Awareness Techniques.
- Continue to look at your "now" body and to visualize your natural body.
- Continue to record your food intake, adding a fourth column entitled "Hunger Level." Record your body's hunger level when you start to eat and when you finish.
- Follow the techniques offered in Week 2 for *one full week* before reading further.

And melt away. . . .

Feedback from
WEEK 2

After having spent a week getting in touch with hunger and recording its levels, you probably have some questions. Here are some of the questions that have come up at EAT sessions at the end of Week 2.

Q. I have to leave for work at 8:30 and I am not always hungry yet. How can I leave the house without eating? I always thought breakfast was the most important meal of the day.

A. If you are not hungry when it is time to go to work, don't eat. Your body is telling you that it is not ready to eat at that time. Remember, you are learning to trust your body. I strongly doubt that there will be any serious consequences if you don't eat for two or three hours. If your body is not sending you hunger signals at "breakfast time," then eating every day upon rising is probably important only to your mother or your elementary school nurse. Your body's needs aren't dictated by clocks.

Most people find they can take a break within a couple of hours after starting work. If you are hungry then, eat. If not, wait until lunchtime, or the break after that. You don't know when you will get hungry again. Eating now because you may be hungry later is a definite abuse of your body. Stay in the present and trust your body.

It may help relieve your panic to remember that you do not live on a desert island. Chances are you will be within walking distance of some kind of food store or other. If not, or if this kind of store doesn't appeal to you, you can always put fruit or cheese or cookies, or anything else you like, in a bag and take it with you so that you will never be caught without food. Then again, I would be willing to guarantee that you will not starve to death if you postpone eating until you are hungry. Remember, you are learning to trust your body. One of the strongest hindrances to regaining your natural form is a regime or routine of any kind imposed by the mind, the reason being that it keeps you out of touch with the present. How can you be in touch with what's happening now if you have already decided you must eat a "good breakfast" before 8:30 every morning?

Q. I'm not certain if what I am feeling is a 4, a 5 or a 6. How can I tell for sure?

A. This is something you will need to learn from experience. We are very new to this game of eating relative to hunger, and we need to relearn everything from scratch. If you feel you are stopping at a 5 most of the time and after a few weeks nothing is melting away, your 5 is probably a 6 or even higher. If you are *at all* uncomfortable after eating, you have eaten past a 5. If you are feeling light but comfortable, you are at a 4. As you put more non-judgmental attention into matching your hunger-level number with your feeling, you will become more accurate and your body will begin to take more responsibility for when and how much you eat.

Q. I got to a 5 and wanted to go on eating more anyhow. What shall I do?

A. It takes your mind time to learn that you are no longer overeating. Put your fork down and wait twenty minutes. If at that time you decide to stop eating, save the food until the next time you are hungry. Remember, you have the freedom to eat later if your body wants to. The more often you experience the light, comfortable feeling of a 4 or 5, the faster your body will take responsibility for telling you when to stop eating and the faster you will be without a weight problem.

If you make the decision to keep on eating past a 5, remember you aren't being "bad." You haven't "blown it." Feeling guilty or judging what you did will not help you learn. Focus on the feeling of a 7 or 8 or whatever number you are at at the time. That's how you learn.

Q. I have a family and our dinnertime is at 6:00 P.M. It's the only time our family gets together, and mealtime is very important to us. What if I'm not hungry then?

A. If you are not hungry, don't eat. Sit with your family and have some tea or juice or coffee or nibble at a little food. Mealtime with the family is not an excuse to abuse your body.

So many of us have grown to believe our love for one another is in direct proportion to the amount of food we consume together. It seems to me the importance of getting together as a family is to share love—to communicate. You don't have to overeat in order to do that. Your family will not love you more if you eat when you are not hungry.

This program is actually much less of an imposition on one's family than any conventional diet which either forces one to cook special "low-calorie" foods and serve these somewhat dismal meals to the whole family—even to those who are not dieting—or forces one to cook two separate dinners, one for the dieter and another for the rest of the family.

I have worked with families who have now begun to make that dinner hour a true sharing experience. Whoever is hungry eats, but the eating is incidental to the sharing.

Q. I really love to eat out. My business and social lives seem to revolve around eating at restaurants. With your schedule you must eat out a lot too. How do you handle that?

A. I do dine out frequently—more than I dine at home. I love to eat at home and I love to eat out. I enjoy food now more than ever. It's incredible to have no dietary restrictions. I eat when hungry, stop when comfortable. *I'm free.* Eating has become a *real* pleasure. I don't have a weight problem any more, so what's to handle?

Q. One night I didn't get hungry at dinnertime and didn't feel like eating until 10:00 P.M. Isn't it bad to eat so late at night?

A. Bad according to whom or what? I don't trust the contradictory opinions about what's "bad" or "good." I want to trust only my own body. If you are hungry at 10:00 P.M., eat, and then be sure to notice how your body feels. Without attention to the feeling, you will not receive the feedback you need from your body. If your body is not comfortable when you eat late at night, it will make changes naturally.

Q. I was at a restaurant this week and when I reached a 5 I still had quite a bit of food left on the plate. It wasn't the kind of food I could take home. I ate it because I couldn't stand wasting the money. What can I do about this dilemma?

A. This is a good time to start thinking in terms of priorities. Are the dollars you "saved" by eating the food worth abusing your body for? Would you take a hammer to your body for a couple of bucks? Examine your priorities next time you eat past a 5 because you have already paid for something. You'll pay a lot more in the long run if you continue to eat past 5.

Q. If I have a dinner date, or go to a dinner party where the hostess has gone to a lot of trouble to cook, what can I do if I'm not hungry?

A. Simple. If you're not hungry—don't eat. However, when you know you're going to a special dinner party or have an important dinner date, you might choose to postpone eating during the day so you can be as hungry as possible at dinnertime. This is not the same thing as not allowing yourself to eat because you have to save up your calories. This is merely making a choice about saving up your hunger. It's conceivable you still may not be hungry when the time comes to eat, but you can do your best on these special occasions by not using it all up beforehand.

I have found that when I'm not hungry at a dinner party, if I put a little food on my plate and pick at it, most of the time no one will notice how much I eat or don't eat. If someone does start to make a fuss about how little you are eating, you just might have to make this startling statement: I'm not hungry! That will shake them up, of course. What kind of silly excuse is that for not eating?

Suppose someone bakes a very special birthday cake for you and you really aren't hungry. What do you do? You don't have to be obsessive and shout, "Not one morsel shall pass these lips when I'm above a 4." Take a piece of cake, have a bite or two. One extra bite on rare occasions is probably not going to distort your body. It's constant overeating that abuses and distorts. After a bite or two, you can always say something like, "This is absolutely delicious but I just cannot eat any more right now. May I take it home? I know how much I would enjoy it later."

Most of you would not allow your dinner companion or hostess or mother or husband or wife to batter your body in any other way. Why let them batter it with food? I have never yet heard a legitimate excuse for eating when not hungry. If you think you have one, I'd be very interested in hearing it.

People without a weight problem do not look for reasons to eat when they are not hungry, and they usually do not eat more than makes them comfortable.

The following are some of the experiences and realizations related to me by my clients after one week of recording hunger levels:

"I noticed that several times my stomach just 'turned off' and I didn't want to eat any more. I didn't even feel deprived. I felt free and good about it. I never thought I could experience wanting to stop eating while there was still such good food on my plate."

"I brought my usual half-gallon of Swensen's ice cream to a friend's house (*my* favorite flavor) and when it was served I only ate two or three spoonfuls. I felt as though I had had enough. It was freaky and exhilarating at the same time. I'd *never* done that before."

"I went to my mother's for dinner—the real test. She always prepares my favorites, but I didn't eat past a 5. I was very comfortable and after saying over and over again, 'I've had enough' (she had never heard me say that before so she didn't believe it the first few times), I filled up a container and took it home for my dinner the next night."

"I'm beginning to realize that I enjoy eating even better when I don't keep stuffing food into my mouth. I thought I had to eat a lot of what I liked in order to enjoy it, but that's not so. As a matter of fact, food loses something when you eat too much of it. I'm amazed."

"I didn't go down to a 2 until 5:00 P.M. one day and 3:00 P.M. the next day, and I was already a 2 at 9:00 A.M. the day after. One day I didn't ever go down to a level where I felt it was time to eat. Hunger really is erratic. I felt great, though—no loss of energy or any of the other things I used to tell myself would happen if I didn't eat according to my schedule. This is really fun. I like waking up and having no eating schedule."

The following was a phone conversation with a client.

Client: I really slipped. I drank a lot of champagne and ate way past a 5. I must have been a 10. I ate way too much.

Me: What's your hunger level now?

Client: I still feel uncomfortable and I'm mad at myself because I ate so much.

Me: Stop judging yourself. What's your hunger level now?

Client: How come I overate? I didn't do that all week until last night.

Me: If you drank a lot of champagne maybe you became unconscious of your hunger level for a while. What's your hunger level now?

Client: But I . . .

Me: What is your hunger level *now?*

Client: Oh, my hunger level now? I don't know.

Me: Stop a moment and find out what it is.

Client: It's about a 6.

Me: Well, wait until you get down to a 2 and then it will be time to eat again.

Client: But what happened?

Me: All that happened was you ate to a 10 last night. That is a fact, but it has nothing to do with the present. Only your *present* hunger level can tell you whether or not to eat right now.

This client was so involved in what happened last night she couldn't even *hear* my question, "What is your hunger level now?" let alone get in touch with it. Learning why you ate past a 5 might be of some benefit, but staying in touch with your present hunger level is much more essential. You may not be perfect—at least not immediately. There may be times, in the beginning, when you lose awareness. But getting hung up on what already happened interferes with eliminating your weight problem.

"I feel as though I'm beginning to know the difference between the panic I always had about cleaning the plate and knowing that I can eat again whenever I'm hungry. It's like the difference between being let loose in a room full of gold and being allowed to collect all you can in only three minutes, or having access to the room forever. There is no need to panic. I actually left food on my plate this week and felt good about it. It's very exciting."

"Freedom is being able to put the fork down at a 4 or a 5. Eating without being conscious of what I'm doing is not freedom—it is more like being enslaved."

> Remember
> You can't afford to keep abusing
> your body to please others.

Learning to trust your body is an exciting process. Your body knows when it is getting the right amount of food. When it doesn't want to eat and we keep feeding it anyway, it gets distorted, out of shape, out of sorts. A certain amount of food is needed to maintain your natural shape. What amount? Only your body can tell you.

Go on to Week 3.

WEEK 3

Things That Keep You Locked in the Past

During the first week of EAT we focused on awakening to the body and the eating process. During the second week, we directed our attention to hunger levels. This week we will explore another area—things that keep us locked in the past.

In the beginning, STAYING IN THE PRESENT may have seemed strange. But after practicing for two weeks it will probably start to seem easier and more natural to you. The importance of staying in the present is obvious. The only time we can "experience"—the only time food actually goes into, or stays out of, our mouths—is right *now*. The more our attention remains in the present, the easier it becomes to make a decision based on our present feelings of hunger or comfort. Many of the techniques you learned the first week are tools for directing attention to the present.

At this point it would be helpful for us to take a look at some of the things that keep us locked into past patterns. It is not necessary to analyze, judge, get angry or, worst of all, to suffer over any of this. Just begin to observe what your mind is saying.

Past Decisions

Basing our lives on past decisions leads to an inflexible, tense, unrealistic and unnatural existence. The decisions to please Mother by cleaning the plate, eating three times a day, never leaving the house without eating breakfast, may or may not have been valid at the time that they were first made. But are they relevant now? Why should we clean our plates *now* because twenty or thirty or fifty years ago it pleased someone else? Even yesterday's decisions may not be valid today.

Each time we are about to put food into our mouths, a *new* decision needs to be made, based solely on our hunger level at that moment. It is far more exciting to live in the present than to live mechanically by rules made years and years ago. Keeping attention in the present makes for a much more zestful, interesting life.

Begin to observe what past decisions interfere with current ones. Don't *try* to change those decisions and make new ones to live by. Don't *try* to exchange your old behavioral patterns for new ones. Just become aware of those past decisions by observing what your mind is telling you, and then turning your attention back to the present. For instance, the mind might say: "Keep eating —there's still food on the plate." That would be a good time to check in with your hunger level. The decision to clean the plate was made some time in the past. Whether or not to keep eating is a matter to be decided on the basis of your *present* hunger level. Attending to the "now" will not allow past decisions to interfere with your body's messages or your enjoyment of the moment at hand. Choose to live in the present.

Automatic Reactions

How often we react like automatons. What happens when we are unhappy? We need a reward to make us feel better—a hot fudge sundae or a piece of candy. After all, don't we deserve it? Isn't that what we were given to soothe us as children? Poor Johnny. Does your boo-boo hurt? Have a cookie. Poor Susie. Did the doctor hurt you with his needle? Have a lollipop.

On the other hand, when there is occasion for rejoicing, or when we have been good little girls or boys, we get the same reward. Be good and you can have a candy bar. Eat all your dinner and you can have dessert. You've been so good all day, you can have an ice cream cone. We are conditioned to behave like Pavlov's dogs. With regard to food, so many of us are still enslaved to the messages we got at the age of two, even though they may have little application to our present circumstances.

Each of us has our own automatic reactions to emotions and situations, our own special Pavlovian responses to boredom, fatigue, overstimulation, depression, tension, nervousness, loneliness, indecision, excitement, happiness, sadness, insecurity, rage. My own reaction to insecurity was always to have a bowl of oatmeal. Others may find tapioca, chicken soup or potato chips reassuring. What about you? It is fascinating to see how we react to specific emotions.

The time of day also causes us to react automatically. "It's dinnertime, I must be hungry." Someone I know very often says, "It's six o'clock. I'm not hungry, but let's eat and get it over with." If you are at work, hungry or not, break time is a standard signal for doughnuts and coffee, but as you have probably noticed after a week of attention to hunger levels, the time of day may have very little to do with whether or not you are hungry.

And how about the automatic reaction of walking into your mother's house and going right to the refrigerator?

It is not necessary to analyze and try to change each of our reactions one by one. That would take years of intensive work. Eating Awareness Training, by keeping us in the present, will instinctively separate our reactions to the past from our responses to the present. Whenever you feel ingrained reactions taking you away from the "now," turn your attention back to the present. That will make eating a simple matter concerning only your present hunger level.

Past Concepts

Throughout our lifetime we collect thousands of concepts about eating. We have concepts about when to eat, how much we should eat, what we should eat and why we should eat. We also collect concepts about why we are overweight and have to stay there: I have big bones; everything I eat turns to fat (actually, according to the AMA, only 5 percent of obese people have any metabolic or endocrine disorder, the rest simply overeat); my father is fat and I'm built just like him. Concepts seem to give one an immediate, false sense of security. Put it in a box, and the world *seems* simpler.

But concepts act like a veil to our awareness. They blind our vision of "what is."

Notice the concept words that permeate your thoughts and speech. Words like diet, calories, carbohydrates, thin, fat, healthy, unhealthy, lose weight, can't, never, always, usually, time (dinnertime, lunchtime, breakfast time, break time), portion, reward, punishment, abnormal. I'm sure you have many others to contribute. Notice what they are as they enter your mind. These words are signals that you are being a slave to your past concepts. Turn your attention back to the present and they will not interfere with what is happening. Anything that doesn't apply to the feeling of the moment is a concept of the past.

A Hollywood reporter on radio recently said, "Weight is a constant battle—the battle is always there at every meal and will be there for the rest of our lives." This popular concept—that there is no painless solution to the weight problem and we must suffer forever to stay in our natural shapes—is the most destructive of all. Diet consciousness is deeply ingrained and is one of the biggest interferences with the messages of our bodies. Deprive yourself. Don't enjoy yourself. If you are enjoying something, it must be bad for you. A hot fudge sundae may be called "obscene." Someone points to a piece of chocolate mousse pie or some such delicacy and says, "Isn't that awful," giggling like a child talking about something "naughty." One commercial on TV talks about "sinful" desserts. How about the old saying that everything that's fun in life is either illegal, immoral or fattening?

Guilt about eating or being free to enjoy what you want, when you want it, was most likely instilled in us in early childhood, or we may have bought it somewhere else along the line. Those of us with a weight problem continue to buy into every chance to diet, every chance to be deprived, every chance to suffer about eating. And if it costs a lot of money, it's sure to work! We don't believe we can actually enjoy eating and stay in our natural shapes.

When you are responding to the body's hunger, comfort and cravings, eating becomes a complete pleasure, a natural healthy feeling, a joyous, free experience. I firmly believe it is our birthright to be happy—to live without suffering. Part of that birthright is to be able to eat without suffering. Learning the beautiful simplicity of eating when you are hungry, stopping when you are comfortable, and eating what the body craves, will allow you to achieve freedom, stop suffering, and *enjoy*. It is a *simple* process.

Many people don't believe there can be a simple solution to anything. I have a young friend who was taking a graphics design class at a large university. The class was given a problem assignment which wasn't due for three weeks. My friend, who applies the theories of trust and staying in the present to many aspects of life, came up with an excellent solution in a few hours. When he turned in his paper, the professor wouldn't even look at it. He told my friend that it couldn't be any good because he hadn't suffered over it long enough. It had come too easily and he should go back and work on it further. My friend put it in a drawer for three weeks, turned it in on time and got an "A."

I have run across many people who are unwilling to give up their commitment to dieting and suffering. I have a friend whose eyes actually light up whenever he hears of a new diet. It's one of the few things in life that he shows any enthusiasm for. That's when he feels the most secure—when investigating some new diet. Pay special attention to every concept that comes into your mind about dieting, suffering, deprivation and guilt. Don't fight these concepts, or try to reason with them, or even try to understand them. Just notice them and focus your attention on the present.

Very soon you will begin to become aware that the other people in your life are very locked into their concepts. They may even start to drive you crazy. A typical conversation at lunch with a friend could go like this:

Friend: What are you going to order?

You: I think I'll just have some tea. I'm not hungry.

Friend: Oh, I forgot you are doing some new program. But there must be something on the menu that's on your diet.

You: I've told you I'm not on a diet. I'm just not hungry.

Friend: Have a salad. That's not very fattening.

You: I'm not concerned about fattening—I'm just not hungry.

Friend: You won't be eating dinner until late tonight. Maybe a little cottage cheese. That won't hurt you and it will tide you over.

You: I'm not thinking about dinner yet. I'm just not hungry.

Friend: Oh, look, they have a low-cal special. Why don't you try that?

You: I'm not concerned about calories. I'm just not hungry!

Friend: You don't get to eat very much on this new diet, do you?

You: I can eat anything I want. I'm just not hungry!!

Friend: Boy—you sure have willpower!

You: (sigh) . . .

Another typical kind of comment you will probably find yourself exposed to, as you eat a universally nondiet type of food, might be:

Friend: Ha! I thought you were on a diet! Cheating already?

You: I'm not on a diet. I can eat whatever . . .

Your tendency, arising out of great frustration, may be to prove you can eat anything you want and "show them" by stuffing yourself with the most outlandish things possible. Don't abuse your body for anyone. You can't fight other people's concepts. They are just as unshake- able and unbending as yours used to be. They just will not understand that there is a way of eliminating the weight problem naturally, without a diet, without suffer- ing—a way beyond their own expertise. Remember, you are just learning that yourself. There, but for your trust in your body, go you. So do *your* thing. Don't let *their* concepts shake you. Don't allow yourself to react to their lack of understanding. Several months down the road, when it becomes more apparent to them that you have solved your problem, they may respect what you are doing, and even if they don't want to do EAT themselves, they may at least leave you alone.

Past Failures

Most people with a weight problem have tried to do something about it at some point in their lives. But whether they tried shots, pills, weighing or measuring their food, substituting one food for another, fasting, Cambridge, Scarsdale, Beverly Hills, New York, America, Atkins, Pritikin, low-cal or low-carb, throwing up, giving up—according to national statistics, in the long run, a dismal 98 percent failure rate prevails. Even if you can stick to the method for a period of time, only 2 percent of all dieters maintain the weight loss. So we begin to tell ourselves things like "I can *never* stick to anything." "I really blew it again." "Why can't I ever do anything right?" "All that work and nothing to show for it." "I'm really disgusted with myself." We collect our past failures until we begin to believe there is no chance for success. No matter what new method we start, we are preconditioned to failure. And there is a lot of truth to such feelings. These unnatural methods are doomed to failure 98 percent of the time.

This program is different. Even when you eat beyond a 5, it doesn't mean you have "blown it"—that you are a failure. All it is is data for the computer. There is no failure—there is just learning. And that learning, without judgment and interference, will allow you to achieve the success of melting into your natural body and staying there. Trust your body. It will not fail you.

Observe all the thoughts about "failing" that come into your mind. And turn your attention to the present.

How to Deal with the Past and Stay in the Present

How can we deal with all these automatic reactions, past experiences, concepts we have collected, and thoughts about past failures? We *all* have a past. But it's not the fact that we *have* a past that interferes with our learning and enjoyment. It is the fact that we *won't let go of it.*

It still controls us. We hold on to those past decisions, concepts, failures and automatic reactions for dear life. So practice amnesia. Empty your cup of old dirty water and allow it to be filled with fresh, clean water.

For instance, when deciding whether to eat or not, observe the thoughts that enter your mind. Are you thinking about the time of day or calories? Now, for the moment, forget that you know anything about these subjects. You don't know what a calorie is and you don't know what time it is. Time and calories are irrelevant to your decision about when to eat. The only relevant information is: What is your hunger level now?

The Future

When your attention is on the future, on what you are going to do or how you are going to be, you are left with very little attention to do what needs to be done *now*.

I overheard two friends of mine talking at a New Year's Eve party. One said, "The food looks so good but if I eat any more I'll be eating tomorrow morning's calories." The other friend said, "Oh, go ahead. I'm already working on July thirteenth's dinner." *That's* living in the future!

Observe the many thoughts that enter your mind about the future. Making a decision now about the future is just conjecture. You don't know now when you will be hungry, what you will want to eat, or how much food it will require to reach a comfort level. The decisions you make now about future eating will interfere with your ability to keep in touch with your present hunger and comfort levels.

Observing the Mind

We cannot stop the mind from thinking. We are not great yogis, nor do we all care to be. But we *can* stop disruptive thoughts from keeping us locked in the past and interfering with our present performance and learning. Don't engage the mind in debate. We cannot fight the mind; it is too strong. We would lose that battle. We cannot give in to the mind. We would lose in that case, too. The way to keep from being affected by past experiences, decisions, concepts, failures and conjectures is simply to *observe* what the mind is telling you and turn your attention back to the present. When you are in the present, the past and future lose their power over you.

Trying to change can take years. It is a simple matter, however, to turn your attention to the present. When your attention is on your hunger level, it doesn't matter what the mind is trying to say. This is *not* mind over matter—it is matter (the body) over mind.

Don't turn this process of observing the mind into an intense, suffering, analytical procedure. That's another form of war. Simply relax and pay attention. It can actually become quite amusing to observe some of the ridiculous things that pop into your head that have nothing to do with the present situation.

Those who have taken Eating Awareness Training have found it useful to keep a list in their notebooks of all the crazy-making thoughts about eating that pop into their heads. This week, record them, not for the purpose of studying and analyzing them but, again, to increase your awareness that these thoughts are taking you away from making current decisions about eating based on messages from your body. Eliminate the nagging of the mind and the body will perform.

Remember, *simple is beautiful.* When this process becomes complicated, suspect the mind of interference.

Homework for Week 3

- Continue looking at your "now" body.
- Continue visualizing your natural body.

- Continue recording your intake and hunger levels.
- Continue following the Eating Awareness Techniques.
- Record in your notebook decisions, automatic reactions, concepts and thoughts about failures that come from the past and conjectures about the future. Observe the mind taking you away from the present.

Let go. Enjoy. Feel free.

Practice these techniques for *one full week* before reading further.

Feedback from
WEEK 3

I am offering here, as a point of interest for you, some of the questions and reports from my clients after their third week of Eating Awareness Training.

Q. When I'm not hungry at dinnertime and then eat later, or when I eat food high in calories, my husband jumps all over me. He is so used to trying to "help" me with my diets, that he constantly makes comments like "Hey, that's fattening," or "Why are you eating between meals again?" or, "You know you're not supposed to eat that." How can I deal with that?

A. You have to make it very clear to the people who think they are involved with your eating that they are *not* involved with your eating. They do not have permission to interfere with what you are doing. Inform them they are not allowed to say anything to you about eating for the next two months. Then maybe you'll talk with them about it. But until then, anything they say will interfere with what you want to accomplish.

Explain, if you have to, that you are doing a program that is unlike anything you have ever done before and it does not involve any of the rules you have followed in the past.

If you cannot stop them from interfering, you are going to have to block out whatever they are saying. Your first obligation is to your *body*. Have enough confidence and trust in it to ignore all "helpful" comments. Turn a deaf ear to all statements connected with eating, whether they involve nutrition, time, place, diet, calories or anything else these people have dreamed of in their philosophy of eating. Trust only your body.

Q. I always felt strongly that you have to have plans for the future. How can you live without plans?

A. Having plans for the future *is* important. That's one of the reasons I have asked you to visualize your natural body. Understanding that you have a past is also important. But being controlled by the past, or absorbed in the future, is not beneficial in any way. It is an obstacle to your goal. If you keep your attention in the present, without that past/future interference, you are more apt to make decisions that will help you achieve your goal. Living according to the past or future doesn't allow room for the present. So understand that you have a past, have plans for the future, but *stay in the present*.

Q. I've only lost three pounds so far, according to the scale, but my clothes already seem to fit so much looser around the waist. How is that possible?

A. For most people in Eating Awareness Training, there seems to be a noticeable reduction in measurements even before there is a marked change in weight. Remember: you are melting into your *natural* body. You are going to get smaller in places that you may never have before. You are attaining your natural body. It's fun to watch where it begins to melt first . . . and second . . . and third.

Q. I always used to get a headache if I hadn't eaten for a while but in the last couple of weeks I haven't gotten a single one. Is that just a coincidence?

A. I also used to get headaches when I went without eating for a while. But I haven't had one since I have been listening to my body instead of my mind. It's amazing the tricks the mind can play on us.

"All my life I had been stuffing my face as fast as possible. But suddenly I realized why I had been doing it. I thought if I didn't eat everything very fast my brothers would eat all the food and I wouldn't get enough. The problem is that I am now forty-three years old and haven't eaten with my brothers since I was a teenager! I had been reacting to a situation that hasn't existed for years. After this observation, my eating became more relaxed. I wasn't trying to change. I just found myself eating much more slowly, and the fear that there wouldn't be enough food is disappearing."

"I'm beginning to notice a lot of things about my past eating habits, and one habit struck me in particular— probably because it was so subtle and so regular. It was an automatic reaction I had while making my daily run to the bank, which is located in a small shopping mall. As I neared the parking lot, I felt a surge of excitement. I realized that I had experienced this anticipation every day, and it had very little to do with making my deposit. I was going to be near *food*. There is a bakery next to the bank and my routine would be to make a short stop at the bakery, buy a brownie or a doughnut and eat it while standing in line at the bank.

"This time I checked my hunger level and was not hungry. So I went about my business. That was very exciting to me. It seems like a small thing, but there was a sense of liberation at not having to eat something from the bakery unless I was really hungry for it. Of course, if I was really hungry tomorrow, I was free to stop—buy what I wanted to—and eat it—openly—not pretending to myself that I was just waiting in line at the bank so it didn't count."

"A couple of times this week I didn't eat until lunchtime or maybe even a little later. I mean, I skipped breakfast because I just wasn't hungry. And it was okay. I didn't feel as if I was dieting or being terribly disciplined. I just really wasn't hungry enough to eat. My wife and I have always been locked into those 'mealtime' concepts. The clock was our guide for eating. Now, whenever it's 'time to eat,' I hear this little exchange between my mind and body. My mind says, 'It's time to eat,' and my body says, 'Not yet, I'm only a 3.' More and more, my body is winning. It seems silly to be so happy about eating at 11:00 A.M. instead of 9:00 A.M., but it really makes me feel like less of a slave."

"I noticed an absurdly amusing Pavlovian response. It happens when my favorite soap opera comes on TV. For years I have been eating lunch and watching the same program. This week I noticed, as soon as I heard the first three notes of the theme song, a bell rang in my head that said 'lunchtime.' How's that for an automatic reaction? I even started to get up to get something to eat even though I had just finished eating fifteen minutes ago and was still at 5."

"Two or three times this week, after preparing dinner for my family, I sat down to eat with them but didn't feel hungry enough to have anything. I served the dinner, sat with the family, chatted and nibbled at a little food. It was no big deal. Nobody made a fuss as I thought they would. I'm not sure they even noticed. I got hungry a couple of hours later and had something to eat."

"I went to my mother's for a big holiday dinner. Usually I have mixed emotions about this dinner. I look forward to going because I love the food so much. My mother is a great cook. But—I also know I am going to walk away feeling like a hippopotamus. It usually takes two weeks of stringent dieting to get rid of that one night's gorging. This time I went to the dinner, kept in touch with my hunger, ate everything I wanted to, including a few bites of three different cakes, but didn't go above a 5. I felt quite comfortable after dinner. I felt great the next day."

"I am finally beginning to see some of the ways my mind keeps me doing things that are harmful. I think I hate my mind. It is very destructive. I don't feel good about it at all."

> Don't judge the mind. Hating the mind will not help your situation. It will only interfere with what you want to accomplish. The purpose of being aware of the thoughts that keep you locked in the past is to lessen their power over you, not to make you feel negative about yourself.
>
> Just notice what the mind does (with *interest*, not judgment) and turn your attention back to the decision that needs to be made right now. Stay in the present.

"I can't believe how much my thinking is dominated by food! The other day someone asked me for directions and I found myself saying 'Turn left at McDonald's, right at Kentucky Fried Chicken, and then it's three doors past Baskin-Robbins.' When someone mentions a city I have been to, my first recollections are not of the museums or the scenery, but of the great restaurants I discovered there. When I took a moment to really hear myself, I had to laugh."

"I went to my mom's for a family dinner. There were five of us including myself, the twenty-three-year-old baby brother. My mother started to bring the food to the table and I actually sat there in awe! She brought a platter of potatoes that was enough to feed most of the starving children in Europe. I said, 'Mom, isn't that a lot of potatoes?' She replied, 'But I only made a ten-pound sack.' *'Ten pounds!'* I exclaimed, and she explained, 'But I peeled them.' The thing I realized is that she had been serving these vast amounts of food to our family for years and it always looked perfectly okay to me in the past to have a ten-pound platter of potatoes on the table for five people. I'm beginning to notice things like this. My entire outlook is changing—thank God!"

"I was taking my wife and family out to dinner this week and when we were deciding where to go, I realized that my choice of a restaurant had always been based on the quantity of food they served rather than the quality. I went for the nearest all-you-can-eat restaurant, without giving a thought to whether the food would be good or not. But then it hit me that I'm not eating such large quantities any more. The whole thing was ridiculous. It doesn't take two or three trips to the counter to reach a 5. I was making decisions based on what I used to eat. I was then free to decide to go to a restaurant where I really liked the food."

"I don't know if I have lost any weight, because I haven't weighed myself, but I feel lighter. I feel as though I've lost twenty pounds even though I know I couldn't have. I like that light, airy feeling so much more than that stuffed and heavy feeling I used to get with all that extra food. It feels fantastic. I found that it's easy to wait until I'm really hungry to eat, because I don't like to disturb that feeling of being light by putting food into my body."

"I was cooking a huge dinner for a party and found my hand automatically wanting to put food into my mouth.

If I had stopped each time and taken the food to the table my dinner would never have been ready. My hunger level told me I wasn't hungry so I just kept on cooking without eating. I realized how much I would have eaten in the past, unconsciously, while cooking a meal."

It was a real milestone for me when I was carving a twenty-one-pound turkey and realized when I was done that I had not tasted it even once. In the past I would have eaten at least a pound while carving.

"I usually play tennis at a friend's house on Sunday mornings. Last Sunday, when I woke up and realized I was going to play tennis, my mind began automatically to prepare my mouth for the doughnuts and coffee that were always served there. That seemed to be the focus of my attention—not the tennis. I felt my hunger level and realized I was not hungry enough to eat. I was reacting out of habit. It startled me to realize that the food, rather than the tennis, had been of primary importance. After one set of tennis I did feel hungry enough to eat, so I sat down and had one doughnut (as opposed to the two or three I would have habitually eaten on the run in the course of the morning). I seemed to enjoy the *tennis* more that morning."

"I realized the other day that I was eating about half of what I used to eat. However, I was continuing to cook the same portions for myself. After about ten days of doing this it finally dawned on me to cook less. I thought it was funny that I was so used to cooking two lamb chops, for instance, that I continued to cook two, even though I was eating only one. I'm not that slow-witted about anything else."

"Whenever I used to start a diet program I always thought about what I was going to look like in a couple of months and what kind of clothes I would buy. I thought about so many things, so often, that I would frequently forget to diet. I can see now that all the energy I put into the future left me very little energy to do what I needed to do in the present."

"I was deciding whether or not to eat something. I did the hunger-level thing and realized I was not hungry and then noticed I was saying to myself, 'The hell with Molly, I'm going to eat anyway.' I started to eat, then I realized that you didn't care whether I ate or not. You made it clear from the beginning you were not going to look at my notebook. You were not going to tell me how much I should eat or judge how bad I was if I ate too much. That issue was going to be between me and my body, and only my own body was going to eliminate my weight problem. My desire to eat disappeared. It was frustrating at first to have nobody to get mad at or rebel against."

It is very hard for some people to assume responsibility for their lives and their bodies. They always look around for someone to tell them whether they've been bad or good—for someone to take the responsibility for solving, or not solving, their problems, for someone or something to blame. I refuse to take that responsibility for anyone. I will not judge anyone's performance or, if what they want is attention, tell them how incorrigible they are because they ate something they weren't supposed to.

By the end of this book you will have all the techniques necessary to eliminate your *own* weight problem. The problem will be solved when your *own* body assumes responsibility for eating. That is where it belongs. That is the natural function of the body. So don't look for someone to rebel against in this program.

I'm sure each of you has had, by now, some experience of how your mind tries to keep you locked in the past.

Don't let it. You have a choice at all times of where to focus your attention. Keep noticing these automatic reactions, concepts and past decisions.

Marcel Proust said, "A man cannot change . . . while he continues to obey the dictates of the self he has ceased to be."

Let go of the past. Stay in the present.

It is now time to go on to Week 4.

WEEK 4

Fear of Success

By now you may have begun to realize that you are on the verge of eliminating your weight problem. It is also possible that some deep-seated fears have begun to surface as a result of this. We have already discussed the fear of failure, but how about the fear of success? The realization that Eating Awareness Training is working may be accompanied by feelings that are unsettling or frightening, and the source of these feelings may not be obvious to you.

It is rumored that after World War II a Nazi atomic scientist, sought by U.S. and Russian agents, eluded his pursuers by deliberately taking massive doses of a thyroid suppressant that allowed him to hide within a grossly distorted body. Our motives may be less blatant, but we each have our own subconscious reasons for hiding in an unnatural shape and our own fears about successfully attaining our natural body.

Many of us have used a distorted body to excuse behavior we couldn't get away with if we had our natural shape. We can go to a party, sit in a corner, not have to dance with anyone and not have to relate to others as normal human beings. Or we can go to a party and be a complete extrovert—the fat clown. We can avoid serious relationships. We can use our body as an excuse for why people don't like us. If we are successful in achieving our natural shapes, we lose a lot of justification for not facing life.

The well-schooled mind will try anything to sabotage your chances for success. It will invent all sorts of reasons why you should stop paying attention to the body *this* week and continue to perform the way you used to. It might even tell you to go on a diet again. (After all, it feels confident *that* won't work!)

Don't let fear of success spoil your chance for success. Don't let the mind undermine your performance. This week, to increase your awareness of this kind of sabotage, record any subversive thoughts in your notebook as they occur.

The power of attention without judgment will diminish the influence of these rebellious thoughts and will allow you to hear your body's messages more clearly. If you try to do battle with these feelings, chances are you won't win. If you give in to these feelings, chances are you won't win. If you simply notice the excuses your mind is giving you, *you can't lose.*

Fear of Loss

For some, the knowledge that there may be an end to the weight problem is accompanied by a sense of loss—of mourning over the problem that has been so much a part of us for so many years. Although we can remember saying thousands of times, "I'd give anything to get rid of this weight problem," when what we thought was a slim possibility starts to become a reality, we begin to miss our familiar, albeit distressing, predicament.

Many people fear any deviation from what they are accustomed to, even if it has brought them misery. One woman said, "I'm used to my suffering. I've learned to live with it. I don't want to change it."

Eliminating a weight problem can be something like divorce. Even if you have been miserable with your spouse, even if you hate each other and know you will be much happier apart, when the time comes to separate, there is a sense of loss. Something is missing from your life, even if it was a pain in the neck.

The same can be true of the weight problem that has been your companion for such a long time. You can actually experience sadness when the weight problem starts slipping out of your life. You can feel disoriented— sort of empty—and even grieve over the loss of something that has been a way of life for so long.

The best way to deal with it is simply to be aware that it is happening and to keep your attention in the present. Writing your thoughts in your notebook will help decrease their interference and may even reveal the absurdity of such fears.

Don't let this sense of loss get in the way. Keep your attention on the decisions you need to make at the moment. The feeling of loss may seem intense, but it will pass very quickly. After all, it doesn't have much weight to back it up.

Freedom

This is a good time to begin to really recognize differences in your eating. This process of change can be so subtle at times that, unless you stop a moment and take stock, you may miss some of the significant things that are happening in your life.

Occasionally, when I meet with a client and ask, "What's been happening to you this week?" The answer is, "Well, I'm not sure anything really happened."

Upon further questioning, it comes to light that several noteworthy events have occurred. Three times during the week one client went to dinner, ordered a meal and, for the first time in his whole life, left food on the plate, or didn't eat at all; twice during the week another client left the house without the "usual breakfast" and didn't care to eat anything until lunchtime, just because there was no sufficient drop in the hunger level (also something that had never occurred before); yet another client had another experience of *freedom* that was never felt before.

Freedom is an incredibly exhilarating feeling. It is about this time that some of you will realize that, without dieting, without deprivation, without emotional, mental, or physical suffering, not only are you not gaining weight but (is this a miracle?) you are also beginning the process of melting into your natural shape. What did you expect? That's what being without a weight problem is all about!

Begin to recognize the extraordinary things that are happening to you. Each experience brings satisfaction and delight and each merits observation. It is very gratifying just to be able to say, "I'm not on a diet; I can eat anything, any time I want to, and not gain weight." Realizing that there *is* an end to this problem brings a feeling of great relief and astonishment. Relish each experience, each time you are not being a slave to the past, each time you are not compelled to eat when you are not hungry, each time you experience simplicity, pleasure and that glorious freedom. Really enjoy these moments. They will become more and more frequent and will soon be your way of life.

Learning What the Body Wants to Eat

Cravings

Many weight-loss programs entice their customers with the promise "We can help you overcome your cravings." Why is it assumed that overcoming cravings is desirable? EAT will allow you to *satisfy* your cravings—with the important difference that they will be the cravings of your body rather than your mind.

The other day I heard a well-known radio talk-show host discussing weight with a guest. (Talk shows seem to concentrate at least half their time on the weight problem.) His comment was, "I know how to control weight: If it tastes good—don't eat it!" When I had a weight problem, I thought the same way. But now, when I hear ideas like these, I am appalled by their ridiculousness.

We have convinced ourselves that we cannot enjoy food and stay in our natural shapes. Why do we think we must suffer? Why do we think if we really crave something, it must be "bad"? It seems more sensible that the natural order of events is to crave and to satisfy. That is the way the mechanism was built. Signals of need, signals of fulfillment. Crave and satisfy.

> "Yes, but if I ate what I craved, all I would eat is hot fudge sundaes and I would weigh three hundred pounds."
>
> "Yes, but my cravings would tell me to eat all the wrong foods."
>
> "Yes, but I'd never eat anything but pasta if I indulged my cravings and in no time I'd look like an elephant."

All of that might be true if you set about to satisfy the cravings of the mind. But I haven't known of a body yet that craves only sundaes and pasta. When you feed the mind you are feeding illusion, and creating a shape that looks unnatural. When you feed the body, you are feeding reality, which is much more satisfying, and the result is a natural shape.

Obviously, what we want to learn to do is listen to, and satisfy, the cravings of the body. The body can and will tell you what it needs to eat. Perhaps you have already started to have some experiences in this area during the past three weeks and have begun to notice cravings, sometimes even for foods you are unaccustomed to eating.

On occasion I have surprised myself by even craving cottage cheese. I used to hate cottage cheese (perhaps resent is a better description) because it represented all the times in my life I couldn't have the hashed brown potatoes.

A couple of years ago I had bronchitis and ran a high fever for several days. When the fever broke, I had a craving for bacon. Bacon is something I hadn't craved since I started paying attention to my body. During my illness I couldn't go to the store and wasn't able to get the bacon my body craved. Two days later, I went to the post office and, after ordering stamps, fainted at the feet of the post office clerk. It was the first time in my life I had ever fainted. My doctor told me I had been dehydrated. He said I should have been eating something very salty like bacon. Had I heeded my body's message, I could have prevented a very frightening experience. (The clerk later told me I had fainted right after he said, "That will be $4.65." He had never before seen such an extreme reaction to the increased price of postage.) Although this is a drastic example, the body *can* give you this kind of message every day about what foods it needs to keep it in good natural shape.

I recall one of those fad diets I was on some years ago which consisted of only meat and water. You could have as much meat as you wanted and had to drink many glasses of water per day. When I started this diet I thought I would really miss having sweets. My actual experience was very different. After about two weeks of this radical eating, I could have killed for a piece of lettuce. All I could think about was salad. That really surprised me. And that was before I was even listening.

The cravings of the body must be trusted. The body knows what it needs to eat, when it needs to eat, and how much it needs to eat. I have previously mentioned the tests using conveyor belts of food to see what children would choose to eat of their own free will. We seem to have drifted light-years away from being that closely in touch with our bodies and from allowing ourselves to exercise that kind of free choice. It is quite enchanting to be able to respond as those children did, as we were meant to respond.

To Satisfy or Not to Satisfy

We have all heard a great deal of talk about "innovative" ways of suppressing the appetite. But I have found that the most natural and efficient appetite suppressant is food —the particular food that will satisfy the body's cravings.

Most people think if they had the freedom to eat the foods they really wanted to eat, the foods they "loved," they would never stop eating until they reached the point of explosion. Again it depends on whether you're feeding the body or the mind. If we eat the foods that truly satisfy us, we well tend to eat much less. For instance, how much cottage cheese would it take to satisfy the craving for one slice of pizza? Needless to say, there is no amount —large or small—that would work. Yet what do most of us do? We eat the cottage cheese instead of the pizza because we have been taught that cottage cheese is what we "should" eat. We may hate cottage cheese (as I used to think I did), but we convince ourselves it is the right thing to eat. So we decide to be good, eat our cottage cheese, and then we look for something else, and then something else, and then something else. Why? Because it's not pizza. We are not satisfied. We walk around with a nagging, pestering feeling because we have not given our body what it wants.

Knowing we can eat that piece of pizza, and knowing we can eat another piece whenever we are hungry for it, represents freedom. We need only get in touch with our hunger level, order the pizza, eat enough to reach a 4 or 5, and experience satisfaction until we are hungry enough to eat again. The next time we may want cottage cheese, and no amount of pizza will satisfy that craving. The freedom to trust and fulfill the body's cravings ends the fear of deprivation and that panic of "This is my last chance to eat pizza! I won't allow myself to fall off the wagon again for months, so I'd better eat all I can while I can get it!"

You can eat whatever your body craves, whenever it craves it, and still retain your natural shape. Trust your body. It is capable of telling you if it wants bananas or oranges, meats or salads, sweets or sours, proteins or carbohydrates. Stay in touch with your hunger level and you will not overeat. The body is completely trustworthy. Satisfy its cravings.

Choosing Foods

Look at the menu on pages 102–103.

What is your hunger level? If you are not hungry, wait until you are hungry enough to want to eat and then look at the menu again. Read the menu and choose what you want to eat.

After making your choice, ask yourself the following questions: Did you look at the areas of the menu that you are accustomed to noting? Did your eyes automatically go toward the low-cal special? If you usually order a hamburger, did you mechanically check the list of hamburgers to see which one you wanted? Did you look first at desserts—the forbidden fruit—and then go back to low-cal specials, the dreary dishes you have been forcing yourself to order?

Observe what the mind was saying to you as you looked at the menu. Did any thoughts about calories, fattening, nonfattening, healthy, unhealthy, come into your consciousness?

Now, look at the menu again. Free yourself. Put your

attention on the same area of the body as you do when you are getting in touch with your hunger level. Read the menu item by item, slowly, and wait for a response from your body. Feel that there is a string connecting your body with that food. There can actually be a "yes" pull, even a slight lunging sensation, or a "no" response, more like a shutdown feeling.

Practice amnesia. You do not know what kind of person you are where food is concerned. You do not know what is good for you, what you usually like or what you always order. Eliminate the words "always," "never," "usually" from your decision. Let yourself have a fresh response to every food. Do not base your selection on old data like "I'm the kind of person who never eats vegetables," or "I never have anything but thousand island dressing," or "Oh, no, I can't ever eat desserts."

For twenty-five years I never had anything but thousand island dressing on my salad unless I was on a diet that didn't let me have it. Now I find that I choose many different dressings. The first time I ordered blue cheese dressing I felt as though I were breaking out of a mold, becoming free and independent. I was actually quite excited about this event. I had made a monumental decision.

You are free to eat anything on the menu. There will be no repercussions if your choice represents what your body wants to eat. Trust your body.

Now, what have you decided to eat? Is it different from your original decision? Take some time to feel the response from your body. Do not go out of your way to choose something different from what you normally would. Don't be deliberately contrary. Just give the body a chance to respond.

If at the moment you cannot get in touch with what you want to eat, there is a possibility that you are not really hungry. Recheck your hunger level. If you are at a 2 and still can't feel a response to any particular food,

DINNERS

including soup or salad and choice
of baked potato, french fries or rice

Golden Fried Chicken
Roast Turkey with Stuffing
Roast Prime Rib of Beef
Hamburger Steak
Top Sirloin Steak
Baby Beef Liver with Onions
Center Cut Pork Chops
Roast Leg of Lamb
Barbecued Beef or Pork Ribs

Fish and Chips
Fried Shrimp
Red Snapper
Lobster
Salmon Steak
Halibut Steak

Spaghetti with Meat Balls
Baked Lasagne
Veal Parmigiana
Fettuccini Alfredo
Sausage with Peppers

SALADS

Chef's Salad—lettuce, tomato, egg, ham, turkey, cheese
Tuna Salad—tomato stuffed with tuna, egg, lettuce
Chicken Salad—tomato stuffed with
chicken salad, egg, lettuce
Fruit Salad with Cottage Cheese or Sherbet
Spinach Salad with Bacon Dressing

SOUPS

Clam Chowder
Vegetable
Split Pea

Chicken with Noodles
Minestrone
Lentil

SANDWICHES

Hamburger
Tuna Salad

Week 4

Chicken Salad
Corned Beef
Avocado with Sprouts and Tomato
Grilled Cheese
Egg Salad
Ham and Cheese
Bacon, Tomato, Lettuce
Club Sandwich
Barbecued Beef
Hot Roast Beef (potatoes, gravy)
Hot Turkey (potatoes, gravy)

SIDE ORDERS

French Fries
Baked Potato
Potato Salad
Onion Rings
One Egg

Green Salad
Cole Slaw
Cottage Cheese
Fresh Vegetable
of the Day

DESSERTS

Cheese Cake
Cream Pies (Banana, Lemon, Chocolate)
Fruit Pies (Peach, Apple, Berry)
Ice Cream
Custard, Jello, Rice Pudding, Pecan Pie

BEVERAGES

Hot Coffee
Hot Tea
Milk
Coke or Tab
Fruit Juices

Iced Coffee
Iced Tea
Chocolate Milk
Beer, Wine

LOW-CAL SPECIALS

Broiled Hamburger Patty, Lettuce and
Tomato (no dressing), low-fat Cottage
Cheese, Peach Half (unsweetened)

Broiled Halibut Steak, low-fat Cottage
Cheese, Melba Toast (no butter),
Jello Cubes

go ahead and make a choice. Then notice, while you are eating, if you are being satisfied.

Make your decisions about what to eat as much in the present as possible. Try to have a variety of foods on hand to choose from. If there is absolutely nothing available that will satisfy you, you can elect to wait until what you want is available, or, if you must eat right away, be aware of the added danger of eating above your comfort level. Increase your focus on your hunger level to avoid abusing your body.

Abandon

Feel a sense of abandon.

Notice the thoughts that enter your mind when you are about to select a food. Are you worrying about calories, or about what people will think of you for eating spaghetti for breakfast? What you need to do is to *let go* of all those automatic thoughts connected with what you usually eat, all your hard-learned "knowledge" about calories, healthy, unhealthy, or proper.

Keep your attention on the responses of the body. Do not try to find new patterns regarding the kinds of food you are craving. Make each decision a new decision. Just because you crave peanut butter for three days doesn't mean you will want it on the fourth. Every day is different.

Just let go! Take the risk. Feel that sense of freedom and adventure—even recklessness.

If you have a physical problem and your physician has advised you not to eat a specific food, you are still free to practice abandon, with the exception of your particular restriction. For instance, if you are a diabetic and are not allowed sugar, your choices can include anything *but* sugar. Or if you are allergic to milk products, you have the freedom to choose from any food other than milk products. It's like moving the lines of a tennis court one foot closer on all four sides. The dimensions of the court are different, but you can play the same game.

Eating what the body wants is very different from what you have been taught. The body does not have concepts about what is suitable for breakfast, lunch or dinner. It doesn't comprehend all those theories about "balanced" meals. Choosing foods based on a response to the body's cravings is a new experience for most, and will probably take some practice. It is a learning process.

Soon after I began paying attention to what my body wanted to eat, I realized that I had been playing clever little tricks in the past regarding selection of foods. Often, in a restaurant, I chose a particular meal because it came with a baked potato. That way, you see, I could eat the illicit food with less guilt. After all, it did come with the dinner! In Mexican restaurants, I always ordered a complete dinner (even though I really don't care much for Mexican entrees). What I really wanted was the rice and beans that came with it. But I ate the whole meal, because it "earned" me what I really wanted.

Then I began to practice abandon. I abandoned all ideas of what constituted a "normal" meal. If all I wanted was the rice and beans, that was all I ordered. If what I wanted was the baked potato, I ordered it along with whatever else I truly wanted—which was sometimes even nothing. I realized how many times in my life I had eaten an entire meal just in order to get to the dessert. If all I want is dessert, why should I put all that extra food into my body? Why mistreat it just because I'd been told so many times as a child, "Eat your dinner and then you can have dessert," or "Nobody eats just chocolate cake for dinner!" Now, if I want, I simply order the dessert. I keep using the word "simply" for a reason. It really is a simple process. Simply eat what the body wants.

I got very strange looks the night my dinner consisted of cream of potato soup, a baked potato and two slices of whole-grain bread. Imagine anyone eating such a peculiar assortment of starchy, fattening foods for dinner! My dinner companions were disconcerted, but I was satisfied. I might never crave that particular dinner again, but it was perfect for me at the time. One of my meal mates mentioned how lucky I was to be one of those blessed few who could eat a dinner like that without worrying about gaining weight. Those who didn't know me when I had a weight problem frequently wonder why such comments evoke my laughter.

But remember that you don't have to prove anything. You are also free to eat cottage cheese or nonfat milk or anything else your body craves at the time. Surprisingly enough, your body may not always choose the foods you once considered taboo.

For us, practicing abandon means eliminating all preconceptions about what is "right" to eat at what time of day. Who was it that first decided sausage was breakfast food? Why is salad or cottage cheese and fruit suitable only for lunch? Because this is accepted. We have been programmed. But what your body wants has nothing to do with what is accepted. If mine wants oatmeal for dinner, that's what I give it. If it wants shrimp cocktail for breakfast, so be it. Since I have been responding to my body's cravings, I very often eat what my previous programming in diet logic would have called bizarre combinations at inappropriate times. I still have no weight problem and I've never felt better in my life.

Food Combinations

Quite a few of the many fad diets are based on a combination of foods that are supposed to interact chemically to result in weight loss. Of course, their originators warn you to follow these diets for only a short time. A longer term is considered dangerous. I would think twice before doing anything for two weeks that might harm me during the third.

I also find it very presumptuous for *anyone* to dictate what specific combination of foods is best for my particular body. One body is different from another, and only your own body knows exactly what combinations are best for it. All we need to do is learn to listen to it and trust it.

Eat any combination of food your body craves. If it doesn't fit someone else's concept, that's their problem. No one else has been able to solve your weight problem yet, so why listen to outsiders? If the waiter looks at you strangely and waits for you to finish giving him your order when your selection deviates from the standard, just smile at him and say, "That will do, thank you." The waiter is not going to solve your weight problem, so why order to suit him? Do not eat to please anyone or anything but your own body. You are no longer going to abuse or distort it to fit anyone's concept—including your own—of what you should eat and when it is appropriate to eat it. Your choices won't necessarily make sense to your mind, but they will make sense to your body, and that is all that matters.

Tell Me What You Eat, Molly

I have had the following conversation with many people who are by now convinced that I no longer have a weight problem.

Them: What do you normally eat in a day?

Me: There is no such thing as normal. I never know until the time comes.

Them: Yes, but what do you usually have for breakfast?

Me: I don't even know if I am going to eat breakfast.

Them: Yes, but what do you eat when you finally eat?

Me: It changes from day to day. I have no "normal" routine or menu. I eat whatever my body craves whenever it is hungry.

Them: Well then (frustrated, and perhaps a bit miffed

because they can't get the expected diet plan from me and are convinced I am keeping it from them), just tell me, what did you eat today?

Of course, I can tell them what I ate on a particular day, but what good will that do *their* body? What I eat has nothing to do with anyone else attaining his or her natural shape—and what you eat has nothing to do with my needs. Every body is different. Pay attention to your own. Listening to the messages from someone else's mind or body is an interference with your own body's messages and makes them less clear to you.

How do I know this is the perfect way to eat? Because for the first time in many years, my physical readings— cholesterol, triglycerides, blood sugar (all of which had been abnormal)—are normal. I've never been healthier in my entire life. And—perhaps still more amazing to someone who felt doomed to a lifelong "weight problem" —I eat what I want, when I want, and never gain weight. My natural shape stays the same. And besides, it makes sense.

Summary—How to Choose Foods

This week, before deciding what to eat, pause for a moment to listen for the message from your body. At first you may not hear a response every time—but give it a chance. Your awareness of your body's messages will increase as you put more attention and practice into this process.

Remember
Attention needs to be free of judgment as to what
is good or bad, healthy or unhealthy, fattening or
nonfattening, proper or improper.

Your body may crave a certain food that is unavailable at the time. After all, you don't always have Lobster Thermidor or blueberry cheesecake in the freezer. If it is inconvenient to go out and buy the foods you are craving, see if you can get in touch with the category they represent. What in the food is your body asking for? Is it the blandness, the protein, the starch, the sugar, the spice, the acidity, the creaminess, the crunchiness, the greenness? Perhaps you can find a suitable substitute. For instance, if you crave a baked potato and it is not available, maybe another bland carbohydrate will suffice. If you crave Lobster Thermidor, what is it in that food that is really appealing to you? Is it the protein? Maybe tuna will do the job. Is it the sauce? Perhaps you can substitute a cream soup. Try your best to find a substitute.

If there is absolutely nothing else available that will satisfy the craving, be aware that this is a danger signal for eating beyond comfort. You may want to keep eating above a 5 because you are not getting exactly what you craved. Increased attention to your hunger level will help avoid abuse of your body. Although it may seem like a very foreign idea to you at present, you may also choose to put off eating until you can have what you really want.

You are also free to choose not to eat, but don't use that freedom as license to abuse your body with habitual deprivation.

Practice amnesia. Forget what you usually eat, what your usual likes and dislikes are.

Practice abandon. Relax and let go of your automatic responses when selecting food.

This week, to help focus your attention on food choices, when recording your intake of food in your notebook, write an "S" for satisfying or a "U" for unsatisfying next to the item of food you have just eaten. Give your body a chance to send you a message. It has been my experience that as long as I am listening to what my body is telling me, I can't go wrong. Trust what is trustworthy.

Have fun with your food choices. Nothing is too bizarre if it satisfies your needs. Don't let anyone's (including your own) tightly locked-in concepts dissuade you from your choices.

Each day brings a new adventure in eating. You have no idea what you will be hungry for.

Take a risk. Relax. Have fun. Feel free.

Homework for Week 4

- Continue looking at your "now" body.
- Continue visualizing your natural body.
- Continue following the Eating Awareness Techniques.
- Continue recording your intake along with the hunger-level numbers.
- When recording your intake, write an "S" for satisfying or a "U" for unsatisfying next to the food you have eaten.
- Record the observations you make about your feelings of freedom.
- Record your thoughts and feelings about fear of success and fear of loss.
- Use the menu to practice listening to the messages from your body about food choices.
- Stop before making a decision about what to eat in order to give your body a chance to respond.
- Practice abandon.
- Practice amnesia.
- Practice the techniques of Week 4 for *one full week* before reading further.

Feedback from

WEEK 4

During the first few meetings with my clients, there are generally many questions arising from this new world of self-awareness they are discovering. After that the number of questions diminishes and emphasis shifts to their experiences from the preceding week. After they have had four weeks of Eating Awareness Training, it is always exciting for me to meet with clients and to hear their experiences. And I would like to share some of them with you.

"I just finished four years of therapy, working on some of the problems that contributed to my being overweight. But while many of the problem areas seem to have been resolved, it had no effect on my weight. When I started this program I was as overweight as ever."

This is not uncommon. Very often, the initial reasons that caused us to hide in a distorted body don't exist any more. In this age of therapy and self-help books, many of us have learned to understand ourselves (at least intellectually) better than ever before, but the actual problem of excess weight seems to linger on. We have become so used to hiding behind our bulk that we simply forget to let go of it. This program will allow you the freedom of letting go of your old, out-of-date body. Why hang on to something you have no use for any more?

"I am someone who uses my body as an excuse for not facing things. It just seems too scary to be thin."

Facing life can be frightening for many people. Doing it all at once, as you are forced to do on any crash weight-loss program, is sometimes too much to handle. Eating Awareness Training allows your body to melt at its own pace. While this is happening, you can perhaps start to face whatever it is you are avoiding—also at your own pace.

"I get mad when I think of all the needless suffering I've undergone over my weight problem just because of all the things I was taught as a child. If I had known before what I've learned in the past few weeks, I could have avoided a lot of pain."

Let go of reproaching the circumstances of your past. I'm not contending that people and circumstances of your past are blameless. I'm not even asking you to forgive them. But persistent censure will keep you locked in the past and interfere with your present experience. Being aware of your past's effect on you is a valuable insight. But, if you continue to live your life according to the past, you have no one to blame but yourself. Let go of the past. Make your decisions based on present circumstances and feelings. Let your body assume full responsibility for eating.

"I've been noticing that my consumption of alcohol is changing. I haven't tried to drink less, but I seem to be cutting down all the same. It just seems to be happening. Where I used to have four or five drinks, I'm having only two. I still enjoy the taste of the wine I have with dinner, but I feel like I've had enough after a couple of glasses."

> I've heard this report from more than one client. Awareness often spills over into other areas of previous overindulgence.

"I don't seem to be able to connect very often with what my body wants to eat. I could only do it a couple of times this week."

> You are learning a new skill. You may not be perfect the first week. Listening to the body takes practice, and, as with any skill, the more you practice the more proficient you will become. Keep giving the body its chance and the messages will become more frequent.

"Choosing foods has been a ball. I found that I wanted to eat cream cheese and rye bread for three days. I never used to allow myself to eat cream cheese because I'd read that dairy products cause mucus, but it hasn't had any adverse effects on me so far, and it satisfied me so much that I hardly ate anything else those three days. The fourth day, however, I really wanted salad and so that's what I ate. I don't think I've ever allowed myself such freedom. I'm one of those people who reads a whole nutrition book before I combine two foods. But somehow, in spite of all my years of study, I have developed terrible digestive problems. When I listened to my body last week my digestion seemed okay even though I caught my mind giving me lectures about what I was eating."

"I went to my favorite rib restaurant and for the first time in ten years did not order the ribs. I always eat the ribs when I go there. I stopped, looked at the menu (I hadn't even looked at the menu in nine years) and decided I wanted chicken. It felt almost risqué."

"I had company and served lemon pie, which is my very favorite dessert. Half of the pie was left over and I put it in my refrigerator, where it stayed—untouched— for four days. I didn't want to eat lemon pie during all that time. Before EAT, it would have been gone in ten minutes. In fact, it never would have made it into the refrigerator."

"The other night, after a meeting, my friends and I all went to a coffee shop for a snack. All the way there I kept saying, 'I really want some tapioca pudding. I hope they have tapioca pudding at this restaurant.' When I got there, I anxiously asked the waitress if they had it and she said they did. I then made a connection with my body as to what it would be like to eat tapioca pudding right away and after making such a fuss, said, 'Actually, that's not what I really want after all. I want a Caesar salad.' It was wonderful—just what I wanted to eat."

That's really staying in the present.

"I have been noticing that everything tastes saltier than it used to. Even when I am eating the same food as everyone else at the table, I am the only one who comments on its saltiness. Interestingly enough, I have high blood pressure and I'm not supposed to eat much salt, so it works out fine."

This has not been an uncommon reaction to salt for those clients who have a tendency to retain water. The body is simply giving you the message "I don't want salt." It's probably not a new message, but you didn't hear it in the past. Start listening for other messages. They are trustworthy.

"I made an effort to find out what my body wanted to eat this week and, strangely enough, it didn't want any meat at all. Up until then I was the sort of person who thought I had to have red meat at every meal, but all I wanted this week was chicken and fish. I kept thinking I was going to want beef at the next meal but when it came time to eat, something said 'no.' It will be interesting to see when I am going to want red meat again."

"I'm a vegetarian, and, of all things, what I wanted most this week was tuna fish. I couldn't believe it. It was haunting me—tuna fish, tuna fish, tuna fish. I finally broke down and had some and it was terrific. I loved it. After I ate it, the nagging went away and now I don't want it any more."

> I have worked with more than one vegetarian who uncovered a similar craving, and it often was for tuna fish. Some of the vegetarians decided to go ahead and eat it and others decided not to. But even those who didn't at least realized that something must be missing from their present intake of food. They experimented with protein-substitute foods to satisfy that craving.

"For years, I have always had grapefruit juice in the morning. The minute I got up, I would have my grapefruit juice. But three or four mornings this week I didn't want it. As a matter of fact, I didn't want anything, and when I finally did get hungry, it was not for grapefruit juice. I don't even remember how that habit of grapefruit juice began, but it surprised me to discover that I didn't want it, didn't need it, and actually had a choice."

"I always eat baked potatoes. I thought it was one of my favorites. This week I came to the conclusion that it was the butter and sour cream on top of the potato that I really wanted. The potato wasn't the thing I wanted at all. I started to put just a little potato on each forkful along with more sour cream and butter. I ate only about one-quarter of the potato and was completely satisfied."

I have found the same thing true of chocolate sundaes. I noticed I really didn't care that much for the ice cream. It is the chocolate fudge that I want. Now, I can have one teaspoon of chocolate fudge and it satisfies me. What is the point of eating a lot of food you don't want just to get the food you do want? If all you want is cream cheese or peanut butter, you don't need to eat the bread underneath it. You are free to eat just what you want.

"I wanted something sweet. I went into a small corner market to buy something. I walked up and down the aisles looking for what I wanted to eat. After I ran out of aisles and nothing created a response in me, it dawned on me that I didn't want anything at all. I walked out of the store without buying anything. Now that's incredible."

Not really. I often hear the very same report from other clients.

"Every morning, on the way to work, I stop at the doughnut shop and have two or three doughnuts with my coffee and read my morning paper. The doughnuts are freshly baked and smell fantastic. Now, of course, I don't read the paper and eat at the same time so that's out. A couple of mornings this week, when I stopped, I knew I wasn't really hungry. I didn't want doughnuts. I just wanted coffee. On the mornings I did want dough-nuts, one was enough."

"I was invited to someone's home after a golf game and the hostess put out a spread of cheese, wine and crackers. I didn't want any of the food and wasn't into drinking the wine either. So I didn't. That sounds like a simple statement, but I had been in that situation many times in the past and always had some of whatever was put out on the table. I felt so free that I could choose to eat nothing."

To eat or not to eat. You have the freedom to choose.

"I took my vacation in a small town, where the food was abominable. It was three days later when I realized that I was eating beyond a 5. I finally realized what was happening—I wasn't going to be satisfied until I got home again, so why overeat just because the food was bad? That doesn't make sense. Even though it took me three days to figure it all out, I guess that's better than never."

"I still have trouble stopping at a 5 sometimes. When something tastes good, I want to keep tasting it."

The battle of taste versus hunger might continue for a while for some of you. We are victims of past deprivations. Every time we were on diets (which might have constituted a great part of our lives), we were not allowed foods that tasted good. Therefore, when we do decide to "cheat" and eat something tasty, we don't ever want to stop. We might never have it again.

As your experience begins to teach you, and you begin to trust, that you can eat whatever and whatever you want, and that taste actually diminishes when you pass your comfort level, you will want to stop when your body says "enough." That may be hard to believe right now, but start noticing it. Keep your attention only on eating. It will increase the taste enjoyment.

If you still feel you really will be missing something and absolutely must keep tasting even though you are at a 5, go ahead and have one or two more bites. An extra bite or two on rare occasions is not going to seriously distort your body. It is the consistency with which we overeat that keeps us from our natural shapes. It is important on these occasions to notice how your body feels afterward.

"There's a fringe benefit of this program. I'm saving money! I'm eating about half of what I used to. I used to tell myself, 'If I lose weight I will have to buy new clothes.' That was one of my excuses for not doing it. With the money I save on eating now, I'm going to buy clothes for my new shape."

Go on to Week 5.

WEEK 5

Time and Energy

Now that you are achieving the freedom to eat when and what your body wants, you may have begun to notice that you have considerably more time and energy at your disposal.

Those of us with weight problems have been putting much of our time and energy into: What should I eat? When should I eat? How much should I eat? Why should I eat? When can I eat again? We have studied one diet after another, theory upon theory. We were constantly thinking about new ways to solve our problem and expending a lot of energy on why we couldn't.

As we turn over to the body the questions of *when, what, how much* and *why* we eat, we are left with time and energy on our hands. Now, what do we do with it?

One answer is to start making a list of all the things you ever wanted to do but never thought you had time for. Some people do not have enough activity to fill their lives; others have too much. Whichever group you belong to at the moment, it will be helpful to make that list. What are some of the activities you wished you had time for? What are some of the chores, the details of your life, that never get taken care of?

119

Whether it is basket weaving, playing bridge, learning a new sport, writing a book, tap dancing, putting up shelves, rearranging closets, painting portraits, painting the bathroom, or learning how to sky-dive, write it down. Nothing is too bizarre. Practice abandon. List anything that comes to mind. You are not bound to it. Let go. Have fun with your list. Then, when you are experiencing that vacuum at a time when you would have been eating or thinking about eating, take out your list, pick an item, and start using that time and energy constructively.

What Do I Really Want?

The urges to eat based on emotions, automatic responses and past decisions will probably continue for a while. However, when they occur, and you have checked your hunger level and ascertained that you are not really hungry, you can be sure that the urge to eat is coming from somewhere other than your body, and that eating is not going to alleviate the cause of that urge. It never really did. At such times, sit down and ask yourself, "What do I really want?"

Do not necessarily accept the first few answers to that question. Keep asking, "What do I really want?" One of the most frequent urges to eat comes from fatigue. It is very common to mistake the body's need for rest for a need for food. Or you may discover that the urge to eat came because you were bored and wanted to do something exciting. The urge might have come from suppressed anger and what you really want is to voice it, or to beat a pillow with a stick, if that is the way you handle anger. Or maybe you automatically contemplated eating because you didn't like what you were doing at the moment—working at something tedious, or cleaning house, or visiting your family. You may find that the reason your mind has turned to food is that you really want to reward yourself. If so, *eating when you're not hungry is not a reward—it is a punishment and abuse of the body*. Give yourself a real reward, something you really want. For instance, treat yourself to theater tickets, or free time to read, or something new to wear.

Keep asking, "What do I really want?" Get in touch with what made you think you wanted to eat. What you decide to do about it is your own choice. All I ask you to do is become aware of it. You will be more in touch with reality. You will dispel the illusion that eating is the answer to anything and everything you *think* you want.

To continue to try to satisfy these urges with food is something like trying to treat a ruptured appendix with eye drops. One thing has nothing to do with the other. Food does not cure anything but the body's need for nourishment. To continue to try to cure these many "wants" of your life with food is like pouring salt on a wound. You are not curing anything—you are causing yourself pain.

If your awareness is being overshadowed by an urge to eat that lasts more than one or two days, stop a moment and ask yourself an important question: "What am I getting out of this?"

A client called to report that she had a three-day period when all she thought she wanted to do was eat. She knew she wasn't hungry, but she had this incredible urge to eat. After asking herself, "What do I really want" and "What am I getting out of this?" she realized that what she really wanted to get out of this overeating was some attention from her husband. That—not food— was what was missing from her life at the moment. What she was actually getting out of it was the uncomfortable feeling of overeating. The urge to eat went away with the awareness of its cause, and her effort then went into getting what she really wanted.

Don't suffer over the answers to these questions. Simply become aware of them. Don't judge yourself for wanting. You haven't been "bad" in the past. Only un-aware. Learn to satisfy your emotional wants just as you satisfy the cravings of your body. To do so, you must first be aware of them, and judgment interferes with clarity.

Ask, "What do I really want?" with *interest*. This technique will help you live a more natural life.

Image and Self-Image

Image

We all seem to have an image we try to portray to others. How much energy do you put into wondering what others are thinking about you, into explaining your actions to others, or doing what you think will please them at the expense of not being you? How much energy do you put into your image?

What Will They Think?

When you want to order a banana split or a piece of chocolate cake, do you feel that everyone is looking at you? You have probably looked at others while they were doing the same thing. If you see grossly overweight people with a banana split in front of them, you might think, "That's disgusting! It's no wonder they look the way they do. Look at what they're eating. Must be at least four thousand calories!" And yet, if there is a very thin person eating the same banana split, you might say, "Boy, isn't he (or she) lucky. Look what he's eating, yet he stays so thin."

Many of us who have lived in a distorted body for a length of time have developed ways to avoid negative judgments from others. We have created illusions to avoid being looked upon as "pigs." Have you ever ex-plained to a store clerk, a complete stranger, while buy-ing a variety of goodies to go home and munch on, that you are making those purchases because you are giving a party? One client told me he had a friend who was so concerned about what people thought that she would send herself Candygrams rather than walk into a candy store.

Some clients tell me they have learned to eat so fast that they can finish two helpings to everyone else's one so that no one will regard them as big eaters. And then there are the closet eaters. These people have developed the habit of daintily picking at their food in public, giving the impression of being light eaters, so others can say, "Poor thing, I don't know why he (or she) is so fat. I never see him eat very much."

The shape of the body is directly affected by the amount of food that goes into it. These "delicate eaters" are stuffing themselves somewhere, at some time, or else their shapes would not be distorted. You can fool some of the people all of the time, and all of the people some of the time—but you can't fool the body at all!

The Saga of the Cookie Bowl

One night I was observing a group of people who throughout the course of an evening approached a bowl of cookies on a counter. A few came up, simply took a cookie and ate it. Others looked around to see if anyone was watching, took a few cookies and ate them. One woman took a cookie, put it back, took the cookie, put it back, finally took two cookies at once and shoved them into her mouth, keeping her head turned away from the crowd. Then there was a man who came to the bowl several times and popped a cookie into his mouth so fast, in such a practiced tempo, that I'm sure he was convinced he hadn't eaten it. I know he couldn't have tasted it.

One woman, who was grossly overweight, took the cookie, held it in the palm of her hand so no one could see, and ate it bite by bite, very furtively, cleverly lifting her hand to her face as though making a gesture totally unrelated to cookie eating. That was her way of avoiding the comment "There she goes again, eating cookies. No wonder she never loses any weight." One woman passed the bowl twenty times. Each time she stopped, looked longingly, sighed as though her heart were breaking, turned and walked away. Such a woeful picture.

Then there was the sage of the cookie bowl who went to the counter several times that evening and on each occasion delivered a nonstop dissertation about all the evils of eating cookies. I began to remember my own cookie-bowl routine. I used to spend the whole evening resisting the cookies. I was being so "good." I was so proud of myself. And then, as I was walking out the door, I would stroll by the bowl, take five or six cookies and eat them all the way home.

To think of the subterfuges, self-deceptions and misdirected energies an overweight person suffers just to eat a simple cookie. It says a great deal about image and self-image.

One man told me he went through terrible traumas before going into a store to buy a candy bar. He was extremely overweight and was sure that everyone was looking at him with disgust and judging his lack of willpower. His obsession about what others would think of him made a simple act like buying a candy bar a mortifying experience.

I have noticed that many people act strangely around me. Those who haven't taken my program and know I have something to do with weight loss, have an image of me as a diet teacher. They feel they have to apologize or rationalize when they eat in front of me. They get so self-conscious when eating a cookie, they don't even notice that I'm eating a cookie, too. They feel they have to explain to me why they should or shouldn't be eating the cookie so I won't have an image of them as people who are not doing anything about their weight. I walked into a room the other night and a woman came up to me and said, "Hi, Molly, how are you?" "Fine," I replied, "How are you?" "Fat!" I guess she thought she'd better say it before anyone else did.

The images we try to portray to others and the images we try to hide from ourselves become intermingled, inevitably leading to a very confused self-image. That may be why it is hard for some of you to look in the mirror and see yourselves as you really are. You are more than willing to judge yourself, but not to truly see yourself. For change to happen, you need to have an image that is based not on excuses, but on truth; not on illusion but on reality.

Self-Image

You may have noticed by now that I have not used the word "thin" thus far in the context of EAT. It was a deliberate omission because thin may not be a realistic image for everyone. It may have little to do with your given shape. Having to conform to the idea of thin creates anxiety and frustration that greatly interfere with your ability to achieve what you want, and with your potential to be in the shape you were meant to have. I don't know if you are supposed to be thin. I *do* know that you are supposed to be in your natural shape. Thin may or may not be attainable. Your natural form is. It is a burdensome concept that everyone has to look like a model in a jeans commercial. Let go of your images of "thin." Be in touch with reality, with your natural self. Something within you knows exactly what that is.

Also, in the context of this program, I have not mentioned "losing weight." The image we have of ourselves as *losers* seems to trigger a response that makes us want to run out, as fast as possible, and find what we have lost. No one really wants to lose anything. Losing something has a negative connotation. What we do want is that feeling of melting into our natural forms. "Melting" does not produce the anxiety, frustration, anger and fear that so many of us experience when *losing* weight. The weight that's melting off your body now is weight you will, happily, never look for (or find) again.

Identification

I remember I used to look at a woman with a relatively nice figure and feel longingly curious about what it might be like to have such a shape rather than being constantly absorbed with thoughts about my own size. Shopping for clothes, for instance, was always an agonizing experience. I couldn't imagine what it would be like to walk into a store without always having to search for something to make me look smaller, or to not be disgusted with what I looked like in new clothes. Nor could I imagine how it would feel to head toward the size ten rack and have everything fit. When the time came that my size made it necessary to go to a specialty shop for large women, I began to make my own tent dresses so that I wouldn't need to deal with that problem any more. I thought about how wonderful it would be to walk through life without a care in the world with regard to eating or my size. I guess I was always looking for the freedom that seemed so unattainable, but that turned out to belong to me all along.

I had always identified with people with a weight problem, the people who were constantly discussing weight, diets, calories, new theories about foods, and their "naughty" eating, and who had a comment to make about everything that went into their mouths. Then, lo and behold, somewhere in this process of becoming more aware, those old conversations became tedious and I noticed that I was beginning to identify with the other group—the "lucky" set I had always envied. I realized that, for me, eating had become a simple matter of hunger and comfort and the food my body craved. *My* group was now the one that didn't have a problem about eating. My self-identification had changed completely, even before I had melted completely into my natural shape.

Observing Our Self-Image

Most people with a weight problem would like to be rid of it, but at the same time they want to hang on to their old self-image. This creates quite a dilemma—one that contributes to the yo-yo syndrome.

We all have some image of ourselves. For various reasons that image rarely has anything to do with reality. I asked you, at the beginning of this program, to stand before the mirror and look at your body, without judgments, in order to make your present image more realistically clear to yourself. I also asked you to visualize your natural body. There is more to practicing that technique than just knowing your goal. It's important to become friendly with your natural image. It is the form you are entitled to: your birthright. Many people who lose weight are faced with a body so unfamiliar to them that, rather than stay in that natural, perhaps even svelte, shape, they freak out and scurry back, as quickly as possible, to the old familiar distorted shape—the one that's been their image for so long. "It may not be beautiful, but it's me—*all* me." We seem to take comfort in the familiar and to fear the unfamiliar.

But once you have become intimate with your natural body, you don't have that excuse any longer. You will have had the chance to become familiar, comfortable and friendly with your new body by the time you melt down to it. Keep visualizing your natural form. By the time you actually reach it, your self-image and your real shape will be a matched set.

People who meet me for the first time and find out I used to weigh one hundred eighty-five pounds are completely amazed. I consistently get the same comment: "But you don't look as though you were ever fat!" I'm sure you've seen many people, maybe even yourself, who have lost weight and still look like fat people who are only temporarily thin. One of the reasons I don't look that way is that my self-image has changed so much. I don't see myself as a fat person who got lucky for a while and was able to maintain control. My self-image is, realistically, that of someone who has no weight problem.

I met a woman who belonged to a weight-loss group that taught her, "There is no such thing as an ex-fattie!" When she told me that, her face was contorted and full of anguish. She was taught that she had to constantly think of herself as a fat person who was just *temporarily* thin—that she could never relax with her thinness but must maintain a constant vigil against the possibility of getting fat again. How exhausting! How seemingly impossible! And how different from the way my clients and I feel! We know that we are entitled to our natural shapes. All the things we did to distort them were temporary, and as soon as we let our bodies assume the responsibility for eating, we were never troubled with that problem again. We can relax and enjoy life. We're free.

What images have you formed about your size, about the way you have to dress, about how you have to behave in public, about the way you eat? One of the most locked-in self-images is that of the "dieter." It is difficult for those who have formed this image of themselves to imagine they won't always have to "watch" what they eat.

Another typical self-image is that of the "healthy" eater. These people have spent immeasurable energy assimilating contradictory information from innumerable sources and developing strong images of themselves as "health-food nuts."

If you have either one of these images of yourself, the most difficult part of this program will be in the choice of foods. You, in particular, need to practice abandon when deciding what to eat.

"I'm the Kind of Person Who . . ."

Notice how many times you think, or say, "I'm the kind of person who . . ." It is statements like these that keep us locked into a past self-image and do not allow us to change.

"I'm the kind of person who can't go without breakfast."

"I'm the kind of person who gets a headache if I don't eat."

"I'm the kind of person who can never lose weight."

"I'm the kind of person who never sticks to anything."

"I'm the kind of person who can't visualize anything."

"I'm the kind of person who can't eat like other people."

"I'm the kind of person who never eats vegetables."

"I'm the kind of person who can only wear dark colors."

"I'm the kind of person who will have to diet the rest of my life."

"I'm the kind of person who has to watch every calorie."

"I'm the kind of person . . ."

I remember thinking I was the kind of person who was not dedicated or committed. In retrospect, it would be very difficult to match the commitment I had when I drove all over the city to find German chocolate cake at 1:00 A.M., and that was more than once!

I'm not contending that you are or aren't that "kind of person." I *am* saying that statements of this sort are out of the past.

Changing Your Self-Image

How does one change a self-image? By observing what the mind is telling you about your image, becoming conscious of all thoughts about your image and self-image, and turning your attention to what is happening now. Let go of the past. Do not allow yourself to be locked into your past self-image. I knew someone who lost over one hundred pounds, wore a size seven and still walked through doors sideways trying to gracefully manage the bulk that was no longer there.

You need to stay in the present to keep up with ever-changing experiences and to find out what kind of person you are at the moment, and it's essential to allow that change to occur. You are in the process of changing from someone with a weight problem into being a freedom-eater.

I have worked with many clients who, despite the fact that they are still fifty or more pounds overweight, *know* they have already eliminated their weight problem. It is just a matter of having the body melt away and catch up with what they already know is true for them. They have a completely different and refreshing attitude of freedom toward eating that they had never attained before. But if you keep on living up to your past self-image, you will continue to look as you did in the past—another great piece of sabotage by the mind.

Notice your walk, your carriage, your attitude. As you begin to melt, don't cling to the old way of dressing, walking, or eating in public. If you are the "kind of person" who always wears overblouses, take a risk: break out of the mold and tuck in your blouse or even wear a belt. If you have never worn jeans, stay in the present and notice when your body is ready to wear them. Be reckless. Let go of the distorted image and see what is happening now. Don't let your past self-image compel you to cling to your old shape. Abandon it and find out who you really are. Allow yourself room to change and grow. Don't limit yourself. Get out of your own way and let the *real* you come out. If your self-image is one of having a weight problem for the rest of your life, you'll probably live up to it.

Practice amnesia. Forget what kind of person you were,

what you liked to eat, what you could or couldn't do, or what you usually did. It's exciting to make your decision in the present.

This week, become aware, without judgment, of everything that has to do with image and self-image. Don't agonize or analyze or try to solve problems. Just observe and turn your attention back to the present. Write these thoughts down in your notebook. That will increase your awareness.

Let go of the past. See what the present will bring. Try it. I think you'll like you.

Homework for Week 5

- Continue looking at your "now" body.
- Continue visualizing your natural body.
- Continue to follow Eating Awareness Techniques.
- Continue recording your intake along with hunger levels and "S" or "U" for satisfying or unsatisfying foods.
- Observe your thoughts and feelings about fear of success, fear of loss, and feelings of freedom.
- Continue to give the body a chance to respond to food choices before eating.
- Record thoughts about image and self-image.
- Practice abandon and amnesia.
- Be sure to take *one full week* to practice these techniques before going on.

Feedback from
WEEK 5

After five weeks of EAT clients have asked these questions and made the following observations:

Q. I didn't feel like writing down what I ate this week. I don't know if I've gotten lazy or if it is time to stop. How can I tell?

A. How strong is your awareness of the eating process? If you are maintaining a high level of awareness without recording your intake, then there is no longer any need for this tool. If you stop and then become less aware and are eating or overeating without being conscious of either, then you are not ready to stop writing in your notebook. Only you can tell when it is time to stop without any danger to yourself. To thine own self be true.

Q. I know it's not your intent for me to lose so fast, but I've already lost ten pounds. Is this unusual?

A. I have no intentions nor expectations about how quickly or slowly your body will melt. Some bodies seem to want to melt away in a hurry. I met with a client recently who melted fourteen pounds away in the first two weeks. For others, it may go more slowly. Don't limit yourself in either direction—fast or slow. Let go to the body's wisdom. What is important is that it feels good to you.

Q. I am feeling so good about what's happening that I keep thinking, "It's a miracle! This is too good to be true." Is it really going to last?

A. It seems we tend to believe that "good" things will not last, that we don't deserve them, and that "bad" things will last forever. We go so far as to be afraid to admit that things are going well, for fear they will then change for the worse. It's amazing how long it takes to recover from sorrow and how quickly we recover from joy.

You are now learning to trust something that won't disappear: the potential of your own body. You are *entitled* to a natural shape without suffering. If you stay attentive it will never disappear. Enjoy what's happening. You deserve it. It's up to you.

Q. I've always been into health foods. As for choosing what to eat, I am beginning to feel what my body is telling me at times, but I don't want to eat things with preservatives and white flour and stuff like that. What can I do?

A. I'm not trying to get you to be less discriminating when it comes to preservatives or artificial additives. If your body is craving bread, for instance, it is your choice whether you want to buy white bread with preservatives, or 22-grain bread without. If your body is telling you it wants green vegetables, you can certainly choose to steam a fresh, green, organic vegetable rather than buy canned or frozen ones. All I want you to do is heed the messages of your body. Brand names are strictly your preference.

Q. I went to a fancy restaurant with some people and I wasn't too hungry. What I really wanted was a baked potato with lots of sour cream and chives. How can I bring myself to order only a potato? Things are just not done that way.

A. You can choose to continue to do things as they were done in the past, and chances are you will continue to look as you did in the past. Let go of the image you portray for other people and maybe you can also let go of your excess weight.

Q. At dinnertime each night my husband always carves and serves for the whole family, and he gives each of us large portions. He seems to resent letting us serve ourselves. It's a real problem. What can I do?

A. The circumstances and situations in your life become problems because you start with the premise that you might "have to" eat when you are not hungry— or "have to" eat more than is comfortable. When you start with the premise that there will never be a legitimate reason, excuse, or problem that will make you eat when you are not hungry, or eat beyond your comfort level, it is amazing to discover how easily all the problems are solved. If you think there is no solution, suspect your mind of interference. You can solve all of your eating problems yourself even though your mind will continue to bombard you with problems it would love to make you believe are unsolvable.

For instance, you can let him know as he is serving that you are not hungry and that you want very little food; tell him what foods you are interested in eating; let him serve you and eat what you want and leave the rest; or, if he still makes a fuss when you don't finish your food (or eat any of it), explain that you are not angry at him, you haven't stopped loving him, you don't want a divorce—you simply aren't hungry.

When you are responding to the body and refuse to abuse it for any reason—there are no problems.

"I have become interested in watching other people eat. I was in an Italian restaurant the other night and watched a family of four. I was fascinated. They shoveled the food into their mouths, seemingly without stopping to take a breath, until every morsel was gone. The helpings of food on their plates were huge. I ate only about half of what was on my plate. I'm sure none of them were really tasting anything. They couldn't. There wasn't time. They were eating like robots. It was like a scene from a movie. I realized that there, but for Eating Awareness Training, go I. It is exactly how I used to eat. I've been going to this restaurant for a couple of years and before EAT I don't remember ever leaving anything on the plate. I feel very lucky—and relieved."

"I feel this program has taken all the stress out of eating."

"It's become quite evident to me, while observing my mind about my image, that I have been spending a lot of time worrying about what others are thinking. I caught myself being concerned about the waiter, my friends, and the strangers at the next table. It was a sharp awakening. I took the bull by the horns and ate what *I* really wanted to eat. It was quite a step for me. I liked it a lot."

"My dog got hurt the other day and my mother ran to it with some turkey in her hand—the cure-all! That's exactly how *I* was raised.

"My mother got a box of chocolates, opened it and offered me some. As I was taking one she looked at me and said, 'Shame on you.' I realized what double messages I had received all my life. 'Have some more to eat.' 'Why don't you go on a diet? You're big as a house.' Eat more—but lose weight. It's no wonder I had gotten myself, and my body, in the condition it was in. For the first time, in my life, I was able to watch this scene with interest and not feel my usual devastation."

It does seem that some mothers think their main role is to get us to overeat. I worked with an eighteen-year-old boy whose mother was extremely concerned about his being overweight. When we finished the first session, he started to leave the house and the same mother who was so concerned with her son's weight said, "Honey, have something to eat before you leave." He said, "I'm not hungry, Mom." "But you hardly ate anything today. Why don't you eat something?"

"Until the last couple of weeks, when I would stop to pick up dinner for myself, I would go to McDonald's, order a Big Mac, a McRib and a Chicken McNugget, and when the person behind the counter would say, 'Is that all, sir?' I would think for a moment and say, '*They* didn't tell me if they wanted anything else. I guess I'll take two small fries.' (I figured if I ordered one large one, they would be sure it was all for me, but if I ordered two small ones they'd never know.) I had worked up this whole scenario so they wouldn't look at my body and say, 'No wonder.' I actually used to suffer over what they would think behind the counter at McDonald's!"

"I'm beginning to ask for doggie bags. It makes me feel better not to leave food at the restaurant once I pay for it, so I take it home. It is something I never would do before because I didn't want anyone to consider me cheap or unsophisticated. So I used to eat it all. What a ridiculous solution. Talk about abusing the body for the sake of others. That's exactly what I had been doing. Besides, it's really nice to have such good food in the freezer. I bought some aluminum trays like those for frozen TV dinners, and I make my own little meals. And I'm saving money. I get two meals (at least) for the price of one. I'm not embarrassed any more about asking for the doggie bag. It's my food. I paid for it and I'm entitled to it. They're only going to have to throw it away anyhow. It feels good to be unconcerned about my image and to do what *I* want to do."

"For three days I kept wanting to eat. I knew I wasn't hungry, but something was making me want to eat anyway. Finally I realized that what I really wanted was to be pampered, and my old pattern was to think food would take care of that. So, instead, I took a day off, went to bed, and did nothing that whole day but watch TV and read. It was beautiful! I didn't have to keep cramming food into my body to try to produce a pampered feeling like I would have before I started this program."

"I feel positively dumb. All these years I've been stuffing my face and worrying about my weight for nothing. How come I didn't know this all along?"

You did. You were just taught otherwise.

"I can't believe how little it takes to satisfy me most of the time and I haven't felt that anything has been taken away from me. Sometimes I just have a few bites. Of course, other times I eat more, but I'm so excited about this whole thing. I would never have believed it could be fun to lose weight."

"All week I've been noticing that the people I've been with seem to talk about nothing but new ways to lose weight: diets, the newest pills, fasts, and even floating in tanks to find out about body fat."

After I became conscious of the eating process, I also noticed that most people talk incessantly about this subject—as I once did. All that talk—and no real solution. The best thing you can do when the conversation turns to diets and new ways to lose weight is to close your ears to it before you get caught up in the same old thing. You now know what to trust and how to eliminate your weight problem, so don't get sucked back into old concepts just to be sociable. Give them a copy of Eating Awareness Training instead.

"I used to get very anxious about going places where there would not be any food available for hours. The thought of going for a ride without knowing where the next gas/*food* stop was would make me panicky. This week I had the weird thought that I could even survive a natural disaster without starving. I may get hungry, but there is such a difference between the way I used to feel, bordering on terror, and the way I feel now, free and sort of on top of things."

"Observing thoughts about self-image made me realize that the strongest self-image I have, still, is that of myself when I was in the sixth grade and my mother and grandmother had to take me all over town to find a confirmation dress that would fit me. I was made to feel so different from others. That self-image of a fat little girl, weighing and measuring her cornflakes and milk in the morning, has stayed with me for twenty-five years. That's how I felt about myself. It was surprising to find I still felt sad and lonely, still had the pain."

You can help eliminate these self-images that keep you locked in the past by looking at yourself in the mirror and visualizing your natural body. These techniques will help you base your self-image more on reality—on what is happening now and on what you are really entitled to.

"You've asked me to practice amnesia and to forget the kind of person I am. But I feel it is important to know who I am and what things I like. I want to know what kind of person I am."

I don't want you to lose your identity—only your concepts. The purpose of practicing amnesia is to help you take in new information without blocking the learning process with your own overdose of the past.

"In the past I didn't like raisins and now I like salads inundated with them. It's really strange. I must be craving something in them."

"After being enslaved for so long, being able to sit down and have pasta and not feel guilt-ridden is an event as far as I'm concerned. A joyous occasion."

"I'm learning not to depend on food. Food was my out, my crutch, and a lot of times my friend. I'm depending on myself more and I think it has made me stronger as a person because I removed one of my crutches."

"Since doing EAT I have started to like myself. I feel a sense of fulfillment. Even my relationship with my husband has changed. It's better than it has been for years."

"I have a lot more trust in my body than before and not just in the area of food. I tend to really get wrapped up in my work and that frequently led me to ignore and abuse my body. I can't say that I never abuse my body any more but I'm becoming more and more aware of what I'm doing."

140

"This has been such a mental relief for me. In the past, whenever I've been on a diet, I always had in the back of my mind, 'After I gain the weight back next time—what diet will I go on?' I knew I wouldn't keep it off. But now I really feel I will."

"I'm nineteen and for the first time since I was very young I'm feeling calm because I'm not worried about how my future is going to be. I don't picture myself the same way. In the past, if I ever started to think about the future I would see myself as frustrated and heavy. But not any more. I feel a lot freer knowing that things are right."

"This is fulfilling my ultimate fantasy. No diet—I don't have to listen to anyone. I eat what I want, lose weight, and don't have to feel guilty. I had given up hope. Talk about feeling light, I feel like I'm floating three feet above the ground."

"This whole thing has been such fun I feel there has been a weight lifted off my life."

Go on to Week 6.

WEEK 6

The When, How Much, What and Why

Assuming you have done Eating Awareness Training for the past five weeks, as recommended, practicing the techniques offered *one week at a time*, it will by now have become more natural for you to experience *when, how much, what* and *why* your body wants to eat. That pretty much covers everything you always needed to know about eating to eliminate your weight problem. For your convenience here is a review.

When

When is it natural to eat? It's simple. For the past few weeks you have been attentive to your hunger levels. You have learned the difference between eating based on past decisions, time of day, automatic responses, emotions, activities, and concepts, and eating because your body is telling you it is hungry. By this time, you will have gained enough trust in the natural potential of the body to know that it is capable of giving you reliable messages about hunger. The more trust you gain *in* the body, the less excess weight you will gain *on* the body. The technique

143

of pausing for a moment before any food enters your mouth, and feeling your degree of hunger, is all that you need to do to recognize *when* it is time to eat.

How Much

How do you know how much to eat? It's simple. By being a conscious eater. By attending to your hunger level while you are eating and feeling when you reach a 4 or a 5, you will always know how much food your body wants in order to maintain its natural shape; you will know the difference between feeding the mind and feeding the body. After practicing this technique for a while, the body will tell you to stop eating without your arriving at a specific number. You will become very familiar with the feeling of comfort. Overeating will be so uncomfortable that you won't want to experience it. If you continue to listen to these comfort signals, you will never again distort your natural form.

What

What should you eat? It's simple. Week 4 contains techniques for choosing foods. The body knows what it wants to eat as well as when, why and how much. Trust in it, not in past theories. In the beginning, the messages may not be strong and frequent, but the more attention you give to listening, the more constant and specific they will become. Always stop a moment before eating and give the body a chance to help you choose what to eat. Forget about what you "should" and "shouldn't" be eating. Remember, you are more likely to overeat when your mind is doing the choosing; you won't overeat if you are satisfying the cravings of the body. Keep listening and you will have no problem deciding *what* to eat.

Why

Why should you eat? It's simple. Because the body wants to. Because it needs nourishment. You are learning the difference between the urge to eat and hunger. You are becoming aware of the many concepts that keep you locked in the past, and you are noticing that the reasons you used to have for why you should eat—reasons such as attention grabbing, boredom, frustration, loneliness, anger, stress, time of day, and even happiness—have very little to do with hunger. You are now eating simply because your body wants nourishment. Whenever the decision arises about whether to eat or not to eat, just put your attention on your body and ask yourself, "What is my hunger level?" If it's low enough to indicate that you're hungry, that's a good reason to eat.

What to Do If You Feel Less Aware

Your body is assuming responsibility for eating. That is the end result of Eating Awareness Training. When that happens you will have no eating problems for the rest of your life. But until the body has complete responsibility, your mind may be strong enough to win a few battles along the way. When that happens, you may become less aware of your body. You can't serve two masters.

What should you do if you feel less aware? It's simple. Put more attention into listening to the body—without distractions. Become more conscious of the eating process. You might find it beneficial to reread parts of this book. Also, you can ask yourself the following questions:

Are you letting judgments interfere with clarity?
    Remember, every consideration of good/bad, should/shouldn't, fattening/nonfattening, healthy/ unhealthy, distorts reality and interferes with your awareness.
Are you trusting your body?

Or are you listening to theories, diets, or concepts that your mind is telling you about?

Are you aware of your goal?

Remember, we are eliminating the weight problem, not only the symptom. Symptoms disappear when there is no longer a problem. The symptom of excess weight will not be there when you no longer have a weight problem. If you have become impatient because you have a friend on a crash diet who lost ten pounds last week, remember that it is a good bet (98 to 2) that six months from now your friend will have gained all those pounds back, plus a few, while you will have melted, or will still be melting, into your natural shape. And, while your friend is frantically searching for some new "miracle," you will be free.

Are you staying in the present?

Or are you letting concepts from the past or speculations about the future keep you away from now? Are you letting yourself be distracted from what you are doing at the moment? Don't let all the concepts you have collected through the years prevent you from making decisions based on present circumstances.

Are you stopping to check your hunger level before any food goes into your mouth?

Or are you letting the mind tell you that things are too frantic to take the time? . . . I had a fight with my mother-in-law . . . Work is crazy, I don't have a moment to myself . . . My dog is sick . . . I've got a million things on my mind, etc. . . .

There is never a legitimate excuse for igoring your body. It takes only a split second to find out what your hunger level is. Even during a meal you can stop every so often, put down the fork and check in. All the above excuses—and the innumerable others the mind will produce—have nothing to do with whether or not you are

146

hungry. Don't let the mind do its usual expert job of sabotage.

Are you practicing amnesia?

Are you practicing abandon?

Danger Signals

Notice the situations that arise that seem particularly likely to take your attention away from being a conscious eater.

"My mother came to visit for a week and it thoroughly loused me up."

"Every time I have an argument with my husband (or wife) I get so mad I forget to pay attention."

"I was overtired and just started to eat unconsciously."

"I got so wrapped up with this project at work I was eating without even knowing it."

What your own personal danger signals are, only you know. But whatever they are, the solution is the same—increased attention on the eating process. Become acquainted with the danger signals of your own life. You may want to note them in your notebook. Once you know what they are, increased awareness at those times when they are present will render them harmless.

Applying EAT Skills to Other Aspects of Life

In the past five weeks you have learned specific skills to eliminate your weight problem. These skills are translatable to many other aspects of life.

Trust

You have learned the skill of trusting only what is trustworthy. In the case of eating, it is the body. Whatever activity you are engaged in, find out what is trustworthy. A lot of time and energy are wasted listening to contradictory theories and concepts coming from untrustworthy sources.

Most often, as in the case of eating, the trustworthy source is within yourself.

Where Am I? Where Am I Going?

Know where you are, with clarity. Know where you are going, without anxiety. This skill is an incredible aid to accomplishment. Start applying it to whatever endeavor you are involved in, whether it be work or play.

Attention Without Interference

You have learned the skill of focusing your attention without the interference of judgment and trying, frustration, anxiety, tension, anger or boredom. In all activities, seeing what is happening with as much clarity as possible is an invaluable aid to increasing the ease of learning and the efficiency of performance. For instance, I have found this skill very helpful when playing in a bridge tournament, dancing, adding figures, and writing this book. Wherever your interests lie, practice focusing attention without creating or allowing interference. It will enhance your enjoyment and your performance will naturally improve.

Staying in the Present

Being able to focus on the present, on what is happening now, will enable you to learn and perform to your potential. Those who have had peak performances, whether in sports, music, theater or their careers will say they were "right there." The distractions of the past and future were not interfering with the activity of the present. Look at a friend with fresh interest, without letting preconceptions interfere with what you are seeing now. Even relationships can become freer and more interesting.

Breaking Habits
Over and over again I have been told by those who are starting this program, "But it will take so long to break my old habits—I've been doing things this way for years." It's true. If you *try* to fight the old habits, or give in to them, it will take a long time to break them. But that's not what we are doing. When you don't let the past interfere, when you merely observe what the mind is telling you, notice your automatic reactions, and then focus your attention on the present, basing your decisions on right *now*, habit is not even in the picture. There is nothing to "break." There is just what is happening at the moment. This skill is extraordinarily useful in all areas of your life where you want to learn and grow, respond less automatically, and make your old "habits" less of a hindrance.

Staying in the present makes living your life more relaxed, more efficient, and much more enjoyable.

Amnesia

This is yet another skill that will be helpful to you in other facets of your life. It is the skill that will most help you to stay in the present by enabling you to eliminate the past concepts and theories that are preventing you from making your decisions based on current information. If you approach every experience with a fresh, open feeling, you will learn as easily as a child. Abandon the past.

Observing the Mind

The practice of observing the mind, without fighting or giving in to it, is another invaluable skill which will have become easier and more natural to you by this time. To recognize interference from that "crazymaker" will enable you to ignore all the extraneous instructions and information bombarding you and will allow you to respond to whatever situation confronts you with much more clarity and ease. Certainly this skill can be applied to many circumstances in your life besides eating.

Practice

Practice the skills that you have learned. Start using them in your other activities. They will enhance the quality of your life.

It is your birthright not to suffer over the eating problem and to have a natural body. It is also your birthright not to suffer over living and to live a natural life.

Stress and Other Signals

More and more is being written about stress and its dangers. It is my understanding, as a layperson, that there is stress which is necessary and stress which is not. For instance, if you are swerving your car to prevent an accident, stress causes the adrenalin to flow. You need something extra to be able to respond to the situation. When the danger is over, the stress falls off and things go back to normal.

But the emotional stress we experience in our everyday lives (which seems to be on the increase all the time) doesn't always behave that way. We each have our own stress-inducers. How does the person with a weight problem cope with it? Eat. No matter what the cause of the stress, eating has become the answer. WRONG. Eating not only doesn't relieve the stress, it creates further problems. We add to our lives the emotional problem of being overweight, and there's a good chance we are adding physical problems as well. Furthermore, we have still not relieved the stress. All we have managed to do is to cover it over with food.

Now that your body is assuming responsibility, it won't

150

let you eat when you're not hungry. As a result, when you are under stress, you can't use your old methods any longer. You are going to be one of those lucky ones—way ahead of the game—who will begin to *know* it is stress that is giving you that urge to eat, and you can learn to alleviate it before it does its harm.

Check in with your body every so often. Take some time to feel if there is stress. You might feel tension in the chest area or the neck or back or knees. Attention will give you the necessary messages.

When I sit down to type, I become aware of an area of my neck and shoulder that gets tight. Now that I can feel it in time to relax the area as soon as it tenses, I have been able to eliminate much of the pain I used to suffer from sitting at the typewriter for any length of time.

You can start exploring your body for tension and stress on a regular basis. There are many ways to alleviate stress, and you can read about them in any number of books. You can learn about relaxation exercises and breathing techniques and biofeedback. There are many experts on the subject of relieving stress. How you deal with it is your own choice, but recognizing it before damage is done is a crucial beginning.

Notice other messages the body gives you. You may notice digestive problems you never paid attention to in the past. We can be rather adept at blocking out important signals like aches, pains, and burning sensations. Focus attention on your body and listen to what it is telling you about its different parts. When I first began using Eating Awareness Techniques I noticed I had heartburn regularly—something I was completely unaware of before. It has since disappeared. A few minutes of attention now can sometimes prevent future problems.

"Hey, You Look Great" or, Have Patience with Others

As the people around you start noticing changes in your body, you may find yourself involved in some frustrating exchanges. Here are some examples of the kinds of encounters I had within a three-day period, shortly after I had melted into my natural body.

Friend: Hey, Molly, you look great. What kind of diet are you on?

Me: I'm not on a diet, I . . .

Friend: You've been counting calories, right?

Me: No, I've been doing . . .

Friend: Oh, I know, you're into low carbohydrates again.

Me: No, I've been doing . . .

Friend: One of those positive thinking trips?

Me: No, actually, what I've been doing is . . .

Friend: Well, you certainly look great!
(Turns and walks away.)

Friend: Hey, Molly, you really look great. What have you been giving up mostly?

Me: I haven't given up anything. I'm eating anything I . . .

Friend: (Turns and walks away)

Friend: Hey, Molly, you look great. I've been trying for years. I'm so sick of dieting. I'd give anything to get rid of this weight. Tell me how you did it?

Me: Well, I'm not dieting. I found this way . . .

Friend: Please tell me your secret.

Me: Well, I've found a way to eat everything I want and still stay in this shape. It's fantastic.

Friend: Oh.
(Turns and walks away.)

Friend: Hey, Molly, I can't believe it. You look ten years younger. You've lost so much weight! How did you do it?

Me: Well, I . . .

Friend: I hope you're not on one of those fasts. That liquid protein isn't very safe. Two friends of mine have gotten very sick.

Me: No, as a matter of fact, I . . .

Friend: Well, keep it up. You sure look great.
(Turns and walks away.)

Friend: Hey, Molly, you look great. You must have such willpower.

Me: No, as a matter of fact what I'm doing doesn't require . . .

Friend: Yeah, well, you're lucky you can stick to it. I don't have any willpower.
(Turns and walks away.)

I mention these kinds of encounters because you may have them more frequently than encounters with people who are willing to listen. They can be very frustrating if you don't regard them with a little humor. Be patient. It's just another example of how concepts keep people from hearing information that can help them.

You might also encounter the subconscious resentment that some people hold for those who are solving any problem at all, particularly when the solution is painless. Consciously, your family and friends wish you the best of everything, but it can sometimes be threatening for them to know that someone is solving a problem without suffering. It threatens some people just to recognize that problems are solvable. After all, that means they have fewer excuses for their own unsolved problems. It's especially difficult to admit that there is an easy solution to the heretofore unsolvable weight problem. Being aware of this subconscious resentment might help you deal with otherwise inexplicable reactions from some of your friends.

Also, sometimes friends and family don't like to see us change too much. They are afraid of losing the person they have become accustomed to, the one they have grown to like or love or control. They don't know how to deal with the change and may even start telling you they liked you better when you were heavier. If they are overweight themselves, they may feel lonely. The old misery-loves-company trick. What happened to the person that used to pig out with them while discussing diets?

Even if they themselves are not overweight, they may feel threatened. One client told me a very close (thin) friend of hers was annoyed because my client no longer provided the background that made her look so good. She wanted to be the only one with a good figure. Be aware that you may get this kind of response from some of your friends. And don't let it send you back to your old body just so *they* can feel comfortable with you again. Your health and happiness are more important.

Remember
Do not abuse your body for anyone or anything.

Experience

Many of us go through life missing the beauty of experience. We don't allow ourselves to feel the moment. Experience is really all we have. Life *is* experience and it only happens *now*. You can think about your past experience and speculate about the future, but the only time you can actually *experience* is in the present. Notice the distractions. Stop interfering with the clarity and quality of your own experience. Learn to feel the moment. *Let go* and experience life.

What Now?

For those of you who could not help but read this book all at once:

Now is the time to go back and practice the techniques *one week at a time.* And try not to allow your knowledge of what's coming affect the purity of your experience each week.

For those of you who read this book as recommended, all of the skills necessary to shift responsibility from mind to body are now at your disposal. This is not merely a six-week program which ends with the last page of this book. If you use these skills, they will become part of your life, and you will be free from the deprivation of diets, the confusion of theories, and the pain of overweight for the rest of your life.

We have allowed the mind to control eating for so long that it has become second nature. But eating based on what your body wants is first nature.

Notice how free you are feeling.

Notice how much you enjoy eating.

Remember, simple is beautiful. When the process becomes complicated, suspect the mind of interference.

During the past weeks you have given yourself a chance to experience eating when you are hungry, stopping when you are comfortable, feeling lighter, being less distracted by thoughts about food, and being a FREEDOM-EATER.

ENJOY BEING WITHOUT A WEIGHT PROBLEM!

ENJOY BEING FREE!

AFTERWORD

Because the purpose of this book is to have eating assume its rightful place in your life—thereby permanently eliminating your weight problem—and by definition your excess weight—I don't ask the kind of questions you may find in books that offer temporary solutions. I never ask, "How much weight did you lose?" "How fast?" "Have you gained any back yet?" Instead, I ask:

What are some of the interesting experiences you've had doing EAT?

How about your taste level?

How about your trust level?

How about your enjoyment level?

How about your energy level? How do you feel physically?

How about your freedom level?

What are the biggest changes in your life as a result of Eating Awareness Training?

And the bottom line:

DO YOU STILL FEEL YOU HAVE A WEIGHT PROBLEM?

I am not asking about excess weight. I am asking if eating has begun to assume its rightful place in your life? If it has, the excess weight will melt away.

Those readers who have followed Eating Awareness Training through the past six weeks, ask yourself these questions. Compare your responses to what they might have been six weeks ago, and I think you will be pleased with the difference.

The address for Eating Awareness Training is
P.O. Box 4045
Malibu, CA 90265

ABOUT THE AUTHOR

Molly Groger was born in Cleveland and raised in Hollywood, where, as a child, she danced in vaudeville and the movies. She now operates a private consulting firm in California through which hundreds of chronically overweight people have achieved dramatic and permanent weight loss. In addition to developing *Eating Awareness Training*, she has taught tennis and golf, taught and played professional bridge, and worked with W. Timothy Gallwey at the time when *The Inner Game of Tennis* was published. She lives in Malibu.